The Foreign Investment Debate

The Foreign
Investment Debate

Opening Markets Abroad or
Closing Markets at Home?

Edited by Cynthia A. Beltz

The AEI Press

Publisher for the American Enterprise Institute
WASHINGTON, D.C.

1995

Available in the United States from the AEI Press, c/o Publisher Resources Inc., 1224 Heil Quaker Blvd., P.O. Box 7001, La Vergne, TN 37086-7001. Distributed outside the U.S. by arrangement with Eurospan, 3 Henrietta Street, London WC2E 8LU England.

Library of Congress Cataloging-in-Publication Data

The foreign investment debate / (edited by) Cynthia A. Beltz.
    p.   cm.
    "Based on the AEI conference on foreign investment and conditional national treatment held on July 18, 1994"—Ackn.
    Includes bibliographical references (p.).
    ISBN 0-8447-3886-7. — ISBN 0-8447-3887-5 (pbk.)
    1. Investments, foreign. I. Beltz, Cynthia A. II. American Enterprise Institute for Public Policy Research.
HG4538.F627   1995
332.6'73—dc20   95-18045
                                                CIP

Printed in the United States of America

Contents

Foreword

To understand the dynamics of trade among nations in a world of increasingly porous borders, we must explore the field of international investment. In *The Foreign Investment Debate*, the American Enterprise Institute has made a significant contribution. The contributors to this volume analyze the gradual shift within the U.S. government away from an open-door policy, and toward a policy of conditional national treatment; that is, regulating inward flows of foreign direct investment as a tool for improving market access. Considering the significant role that foreign direct investment plays in the U.S. economy, the disturbing implications of this shift demand our attention.

In the 1980s, the United States became the world's largest host country to foreign direct investment, as well as the largest home country of multinational corporations. Foreign direct investment in the United States more than doubled between 1985 and 1990. Today, however, there is a congressional drive to impose restrictive conditions on foreign firms and to limit access to our market by mandating reciprocity agreements. This approach to opening markets simply does not make economic sense in the present global economy. Kenichi Ohmae said it best:

> When governments are slow to grasp the fact that their role has changed from protecting their people and their natural resource base from outside economic threats to ensuring that their people have the widest range of choice among the best and the cheapest good and services from around the world— when, that is, governments still think and act like the saber-rattling, mercantilist ruling powers of centuries past—they discourage investment and impoverish their people.[1]

Foreign direct investment should be encouraged rather than restricted. It is the engine of growth and innovation that creates measurable benefits for the host country by improving the physical infrastructure, educating and training employees, improving living standards, and introducing new management practices as well as manufacturing techniques. Companies that invest internationally further help to accelerate the transfer of technology and shield the host country against economic downturns.

Our own company, Texas Instruments, invests substantially around the world, giving us firsthand experience of the significant contributions that direct investment makes to local economies. In Taiwan, for example, TI and other multinational companies assisted in the early development and rapid expansion of the country's electronics industry. Today Taiwan is one of the largest exporters of electronic equipment, and the people of Taiwan have become major consumers contributing to world economic growth.

Foreign direct investment also facilitates trade in goods, services, and knowledge. By effectively widening the scope of competition and reducing monopoly power in the host country, foreign direct investment increases domestic productivity and promotes the development of higher-quality, lower-cost products. It also promotes the transfer of technology associated with research activities. The United States, for example, has been able to attract the world's best companies, thereby gaining access to valuable foreign technology within its own borders. Studies have also shown that multinationals conduct R&D activities in all the major markets where they participate, and that R&D per worker is usually higher for affiliates of foreign firms.

Further evidence of the positive results of foreign direct investment is the phenomenal growth currently taking place in East Asia. Over the past decade, the Pacific Rim countries have welcomed investment from around the world with few, if any, restrictions. The primary recipient of foreign investment has been China, where foreign direct investment has increased from $3 billion in 1988 to $25 billion in 1993, while generating economic growth averaging 9 percent per year. Foreign firms have helped fund construction of roads and bridges, have contributed to the education and training of the Chinese work force, and have introduced new technologies to the emerging industrial base. In addition, foreign investments will cushion the Chinese economy from severe recession as companies pump large sums of money into the local markets.

The experience in China parallels the economic development of the United States in the latter part of the 1800s. Heavy inflows of foreign capital, associated primarily with railways and manufacturing, contributed to a twenty-five-year period of 5 percent average GDP growth from 1875 to 1900. It would have been impossible to achieve such a long period of growth without the influx of capital from abroad.

The benefits of foreign direct investment are thus too important to the growth and continued development of the U.S. economy to be used as a crude instrument of foreign economic policy. Emerging countries are currently trying to emulate the successful open-door policies of the United States. Our government should not abandon its long-standing commitment to these policies of unrestricted access. In arguing against mandated reciprocity agreements, AEI's *Foreign Investment Debate* provides much needed guidance for American policy makers in the years ahead.

Jerry R. Junkins
Chairman, President, and CEO
Texas Instruments Incorporated

Acknowledgments

This volume is based on the AEI conference on foreign investment and conditional national treatment held on July 18, 1994. AEI is grateful for the comments of all the participants, as well as to the Sloan Foundation and its generous support for the project. The editor is especially thankful for the ever-faithful and indispensable assistance of AEI's librarian, Evelyn Caldwell, the staff editor Cheryl Weissman, and the research support of Christian Olivier. Jose Alvarez, Claude Barfield, Bennett Caplan, Lester Davis, Kris Hall, Douglas Irwin, Derrick Max, Daniel Price, and Robert Schwartz also provided valuable comments and insights.

Contributors

CYNTHIA A. BELTZ is a research fellow at the American Enterprise Institute. She is the author of *High-Tech Maneuvers: Industrial Policy Lessons of HDTV* and the editor of *Financing Entrepreneurs*. Ms. Beltz's articles on technology and trade policy have appeared in the *New York Times*, the *Los Angeles Times*, the *Washington Times*, the *Journal of Commerce*, *Reason Magazine*, *Regulation*, and *The American Enterprise*. She is a columnist for *Upside*, a magazine for high-technology business executives, and is currently writing *Technology and Jobs*, a study of the ways in which technological progress affects labor markets. Ms. Beltz has testified before the House Budget and Science committees on American living standards and the problems of high-tech targeting.

RICHARD FLORIDA is director of the Center for Economic Development and professor of management and public policy at Carnegie Mellon University's H. John Heinz III School of Public Policy and Management. He also serves as consultant to multinational corporations and federal and state government agencies. Mr. Florida is currently working with the Council on Competitiveness on the development of more effective policies for university-industry-government relationships, and with the American Enterprise Institute on the role of international investment in the transformation of the American economy. He is the author of several books, including *Beyond Mass Production: The Japanese System and Its Transfer to the United States*, cowritten with Martin Kenney, and *The Breakthrough Illusion: Corporate America's Failure to Move from Innovation to Mass Production*.

ELLEN L. FROST was appointed to the new position of counselor to the U.S. Trade Representative in February 1993, reporting directly to Ambassador Mickey Kantor. Before her arrival at USTR, Ms. Frost was a senior fellow at the Institute for International Economics in Washington, D.C. Before joining the institute, she was corporate director for international affairs in the Washington office of United Technologies Corporation. From 1977 to 1981, she was deputy assistant secretary for international economic and technology affairs. She is the author of *For Richer, For Poorer: The New U.S.-Japan Relationship.*

JERRY R. JUNKINS is chairman, president, and CEO of Texas Instruments Incorporated, one of the world's leading high-technology companies. In addition to his TI duties, Mr. Junkins participates in a range of activities in business, government, civic affairs, and education. He is a member of the board of directors of Caterpillar Inc., the Procter & Gamble Company, and 3M. He is also a member of the board of directors of the U.S.-Japan Business Council and the Dallas Citizens Council, and a member of the board of trustees of Southern Methodist University. He is a presidential appointee to the Defense Policy Action Committee on Trade. Mr. Junkins is also a member of the Business Roundtable and the Business Council.

CLYDE V. PRESTOWITZ, JR., is founder and president of the Economic Strategy Institute (ESI), a private, nonprofit research center. He was formerly senior associate at the Carnegie Endowment and a fellow at the Woodrow Wilson International Center for Scholars. From 1981 to 1986, Mr. Prestowitz was successively deputy assistant secretary of commerce, acting assistant secretary of commerce, and counselor to the secretary of commerce. In the latter position, he was the principal policy adviser to the secretary on all aspects of economic relationships between the United States and Japan. Before joining the Commerce Department, Mr. Prestowitz worked with Scott Paper Company and with Egon Zehnder. He was also a U.S. foreign service officer and a reporter with the *Honolulu Star Bulletin.* He is the author of *Trading Places.*

DANIEL M. PRICE is a partner at Powell, Goldstein, Frazer, and Murphy. From 1989 to 1992, he was principal deputy general counsel at the Office of the United States Trade Representative, where he negotiated trade and investment agreements with the former Soviet Union and subsequently the Commonwealth of Independent States, Eastern Europe, and Latin America. Mr. Price also served as USTR's lead negotiator on investment issues in the North American Free Trade talks and as legal adviser on the GATT Uruguay Round investment agreement. Mr. Price served as U.S. deputy agent to the Iran-U.S. Claims Tribunal in the Hague.

1

Introduction

Cynthia A. Beltz

The United States is at an important juncture in its foreign investment policy. Traditionally, the United States has maintained an open
door at home while also promoting investment liberalization abroad.[1]
These efforts have paid off, with other countries moving at an
unprecedented rate to imitate the United States and to reduce barriers to international investment flows. Multilateral and regional agreements have been signed (the Uruguay Round and NAFTA), and unilateral liberalization measures have been taken by a growing number
of countries.[2] At the same time, however, a new movement has been
gaining ground in the United States to manage and impose new conditions on inward flows of investment. At issue is whether we should
use foreign investors in the domestic economy as a trade tool to
"level the playing field" and open markets abroad.

As the world's largest source of foreign direct investment, with a
record outflow of $50 billion in 1993, the United States has much to
gain from the elimination of barriers to cross-border investment. But
our choice of tactics is critical. What goes around can easily come
around, with American multinational corporations the losers if other
countries imitate the United States and respond in kind with new
investment barriers of their own. The boomerang effect of our policies demands that challenges to America's open door be examined in
the context of both long-term U.S. objectives as well as the changing
global economy.

Perhaps the most striking change over the past decade has been
the growth of transnational corporations, which now control roughly
one-third of the world's private assets. Foreign direct investment
(FDI), which is the most frequently used measure to track the significance of these corporations, surged in the 1980s.[3] By 1993, the global stock of FDI reached $2.1 trillion, with annual outflows of $195

1

FIGURE 1–1
GLOBAL FOREIGN DIRECT INVESTMENT, OUTFLOWS, 1980–1993
(billions of dollars)

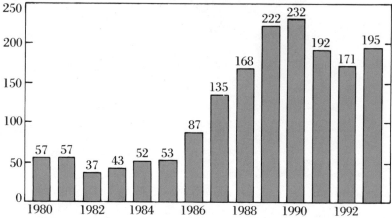

SOURCE: United Nations, *World Investment Report 1994*, p. 12; Department of Commerce, *Foreign Direct Investment Update, 1993*, p. 127.

billion (see figure 1–1). The growth of FDI outflows was particularly rapid in the late 1980s (28.9 percent), growing at three times the rate of trade (9.4 percent) and almost four times the rate of world output (7.7 percent).[4]

These cross-border investment flows are changing the dynamics of competition between firms as well as nations. Instead of arm's-length competition (the cross-border exchange of products), for example, firms increasingly compete head-to-head in local and foreign markets. There are now roughly 26,000 transnational corporations (TNCs) in the major developed nations—triple the number (7,000) in the early 1960s—and a total of 37,000 TNCs that control more than 200,000 foreign affiliates worldwide. Global sales of these affiliates are now more important than exports in the delivery of goods and services to worldwide markets. In 1991 these affiliates generated annual sales of $4.8 trillion, which have increased from an 84 percent share in 1967 to a 150 percent share of world exports (see figure 1–2).[5] Intrafirm trade in transnational firms such as IBM, Texas Instruments, and Toyota Motor Corporation have also increased, accounting for 30 to 50 percent of the cross-border trade flows.[6]

FIGURE 1–2

GLOBAL STOCK OF FOREIGN DIRECT INVESTMENT, TRADE, AND SALES, 1984–1991
(trillions of dollars)

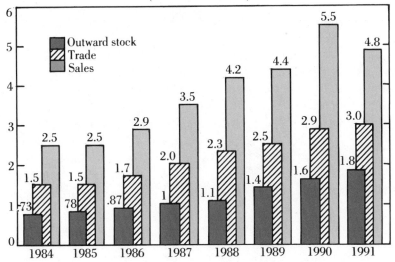

NOTE:"Trade" includes merchandise and service exports and adjusted to exclude intrafirm trade.
SOURCE: United Nations, *World Investment Report 1993*, p. 101; United Nations, *World Investment Report 1994*, p. 19; International Monetary Fund, *Balance of Payments 1991*, part 2, pp. 36, 38; International Monetary Fund, *Balance of Payments*, part 2, pp. 34, 36.

Investment-Trade Cycle

The evidence is clear that both individual firms and nations have much to gain from foreign direct investment. FDI offers host nations new sources of savings (particularly important for saving-deficient economies like that of the United States), advanced technologies, competition, and productivity improvements, while home countries benefit from new export opportunities and the return flows of technology and profits. For a firm, FDI provides a vehicle to limit the risk of exchange-rate shifts, to internalize the international exchange of technology, and to increase global market share.[7] These days corporations must compete not only through size and know-how but also through delivery and local support services that often require FDI. Indeed, few firms can still depend on the home market to maintain a competitive position. A 1991 study by the Conference Board, a New York-based roundtable of business executives, found, for example, that companies with overseas operations had better survival rates. Of the more than 1,500 companies surveyed, those with operations overseas outperformed (in terms of growth and profitability) their domestic rivals in seventeen out of twenty major industry groups. Particularly in the fast-moving high-tech sector, global market share often depends on a firm's ability to establish and maintain a local presence in a foreign market through measures such as production and R&D facilities.

Yet barriers to foreign investment remain in many nations. First there are direct controls imposed on inward FDI, such as restrictions on establishment and on the percentage of permitted foreign ownership. There are also minimum-export, local-content, and other performance requirements that raise costs and curtail corporate flexibility. Second, there are indirect measures—the aspects of a country's regulatory system (competition policy and intellectual property standards, for example) that can curtail a foreign firm's ability to penetrate the local marketplace.[8]

These barriers matter because they restrict competition, the development of international production networks, and the economic benefits of a global marketplace. Take, for example, the link between investment and trade. If they are complementary, as an increasing body of economic literature suggests, transnational investing and the operation of foreign affiliates will generate exports from the home country, which in turn will generate additional flows of international investment and exports.

This international cycle of investment and trade is illustrated in figure 1–3. The importance of the cycle and of international production networks is reflected in the more than 30 percent of trade that is already intrafirm. To the extent that barriers impede the establishment of a foreign affiliate or its successful operation in the local marketplace, trade from the home country can be curtailed. The cross-border exchange of technology within a firm's boundaries is another key part of the international production cycle, with foreign affiliates serving as important listening posts and sources of new technologies for the parent firm. Nearly 80 percent of international payments for royalties and fees (a common measure of technology transfer) take place on an intrafirm basis.[9] Investment barriers thus impede not

4

FIGURE 1–3
CYCLE OF INTERNATIONAL INVESTMENT LINKAGES

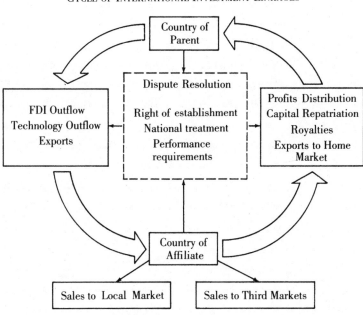

SOURCE: Based on comments from Lester Davis, Commerce Department, and Douglas C. Worth, vice president of government programs, IBM, Statement of the chairman of the OECD Business and Industry Trade Advisory Committee, July 1994.

only the flow of trade and investment, but also the efficiency of the innovation process.

Breaking down the barriers to cross-border investment flows is, as a result, a critical next step in the liberalization process. International negotiations have focused on securing the legal right of establishment, as well as on the protection of an established affiliate from discriminatory government policies and onerous operating conditions. Given the inherent risk and uncertainty of investing in a foreign market, firms need some guarantee that they will have the same rights to invest and expand as their domestic rivals.

National treatment is that guarantee. It is the most basic form of investment protection. It requires that a foreign-owned firm or product be treated no less favorably than domestic-owned companies or goods. The rise of transnational firms and global economies of scale have increased the importance of national treatment, making it an indispensable part of the liberalization process. The rules that are negotiated also have to be enforceable. In particular, transnational investors need third-party dispute-resolution mechanisms, as figure 1–3 illustrates, to settle the inevitable conflicts over entry conditions and investment protection and national treatment. Particularly important is an investor-to-state mechanism whereby the state consents to arbitration initiated by an investor in accordance with an investment treaty.

National Treatment and U.S. Policy

National treatment is a well-established legal standard used in international treaties to open markets and increase trade. The new World Trade Organization (WTO), successor to the GATT, is based on this principle, but a counterpart for investment does not exist. Instead, FDI laws and regulations differ substantially between countries, and there has not been a broad exchange of rights and obligations.[10] Getting from this maze of rules to a comprehensive set of multilateral rules will also not be easy. But there is no alternative, if firms and nations are to take advantage of the ever-growing opportunities from the emerging global marketplace. Indeed, the liberalization of foreign direct investment is the most important issue on the post-Uruguay Round agenda. The task involves not only tearing down existing barriers to investment but also preventing new obstacles from being hurled into the path.

The role of the United States is critical. As an active player in international and regional forums (APEC and OECD), the United States has a unique opportunity to advance the investment agenda to the multilateral level. The United States also has the opportunity to lead the world by example.

From colonial times to the present, the United States has set the standard with an open-investment policy based on the national treatment principle and the perspective that unhindered investment flows are good for both the home and host countries. The United States as a result has extended national treatment to foreign investors in a broad range of policies, resisting restrictive practices beyond those needed for national security in favor of a policy that "welcomes direct investment and supports free and open foreign direct investment among all nations."[11] From the outset, the United States has also rejected a quid pro quo strategy in favor of non-discrimination or the most favored nation (MFN) principle, extending to all foreign investors—whether or not a treaty was in place—guarantees such as national treatment. The basic tenet of U.S. policy is that foreign investors should be accorded the better of national or MFN treatment.

The United States has exported this standard by promoting fair treatment for American investors around the world and negotiating mutually recognized rights and investment obligations. More specifically, the objective is for U.S. investors to receive the most favorable treatment offered by the host country to any investor (foreign or domestic) at the time of establishment and thereafter.

Bilateral investment treaties (BITs), for example, require that a host state treat covered investments no less favorably than the investments of its own nationals (national treatment) or those of nationals of any third country (MFN). Under a BIT, when a country commits itself to granting national treatment to foreign investors, the principle typically applies to all aspects of FDI except for those areas specifically exempted. Performance requirements are usually forbidden as a condition of establishment, expansion, or maintenance of investments. As of the spring of 1995, the United States has signed thirty-four BITs. In the process it not only helped to increase the protection of U.S. investors, but also to establish a body of practice that supports the development of predictable, nondiscriminatory rules for the protection of foreign investors from all countries. U.S. negotiators are now working on the next step—building on the BITs framework and NAFTA to shape a multilateral set of binding rules and obligations. The need and opportunity for multilateral investment rules, as a result, have never been greater.

Conditional National Treatment

The ironic twist is the drift in the United States—in Congress, in particular—toward nationality-based investment barriers. Interest in using foreign investors in the United States as a trade tool has surged as market-access frustrations have climbed in areas like telecommunications and with members of the Pacific Rim, such as Japan. There are also new claims that an open door on investment damages the American economy when other countries open their doors only par-

7

tially to American investors. Hence the argument is made that we should welcome or encourage foreign investment only to the extent that our trading partners do the same.[12]

One managed investment idea is to condition the national treatment of foreign investors on the behavior of their home-country governments. The premise is that the United States has been giving away benefits and getting little in return. It is time, we are told, to have a more discriminating or two-tier investment policy that opens the door wide to some investors but conditions the access of others from countries with offensive investment or trade barriers.

Conditional national treatment (CNT) is the general term for a two-tier investment policy, referring to the treatment of foreign-owned firms that is less favorable than that of domestic firms.[13] It is a useful term because it recognizes that conditioning the treatment of foreign firms in the United States does not ensure reciprocity in any objective sense of the term. (Indeed, the definition of *reciprocity* is a source of endless international disputes.) The conditioning of investment takes two forms: it includes both the general rules that the home-country government must satisfy, such as an "adequate and effective" intellectual property standard, and specific reciprocity conditions. CNT thereby links domestic treatment of a foreign-owned firm to the behavior of the home-country government.

Specific reciprocity is a key dimension of CNT, especially in legislation and proposals dealing with contentious areas such as telecommunications, airline service, and access to international R&D programs.[14] The principle sets up a tit-for-tat test: if the home-country government does not afford an American-owned company "comparable" or "equivalent" opportunities to participate in public R&D programs, for example, then firms from that country will be considered ineligible to participate in U.S. R&D programs.[15]

A CNT policy based on the principle of specific reciprocity thus substitutes a policy of discrimination for an open door. It rejects not only national treatment but the unconditional most favored nation (MFN) principle as well. Instead of according the same treatment to similarly situated investors irrespective of nationality, such a regime promotes both discrimination against foreign-owned firms operating in the United States as well as discrimination between them (conditional MFN).

Some have argued that discrimination is now required and the open-door principles of national treatment and MFN are no longer practical. What is needed, the argument continues, is a policy that promotes inward flows of good investment.[16] But this begs the question of how should *good* be defined?

The standard offered by conditional national treatment and specific reciprocity is somewhat peculiar. Take, for example, access to American R&D programs. Even if a foreign-owned multinational makes significant contributions to the American economy and would otherwise qualify for participation, CNT advocates argue that the United States should consider excluding or placing more onerous requirements on the firm if the home-country government "does not reciprocate in providing U.S.-based MNEs with similar opportunities to invest overseas and derive benefits from those investments."[17] The "good investment" standard under such a regime is therefore defined not by the value of the firm's contributions to the American economy but rather by a political decision on whether the home government's practices are objectionable.

These managed investment ideas demand our attention, even if they are devoid of economic merit, because they are politically appealing. They express in part the general ambivalence that exists toward multinationals of any nationality and the residual distrust of foreign-owned corporations in particular. The general mistrust is reflected in the rising interest in a national-economics benefits test for all firms (domestic and foreign-owned) that wish to participate in government-technology programs. The idea is to guarantee that taxpayers get something for their money from the participating firms, rather than just letting the related technology or production be shipped offshore. The conditional national treatment movement reflects the desire also to impose a performance test on foreign governments in the form of a second eligibility test that firms from that country must pass.

This volume focuses on the conditional national treatment test: should the United States, for example, link issues like access to its R&D programs with its trade objectives of improving market access? As table A–1 indicates, legislation has already moved us in this direction. The CNT principles (discrimination, specific reciprocity, and linkage) have been incorporated into at least four U.S. laws, as well as into twelve legislative proposals during the last session of Congress, in areas ranging from financial services to R&D in aerospace and energy technologies. Before the Manton amendment, however, CNT initiatives and the broader challenge to America's open door received little attention before the CNT language was incorporated into American law.

The Manton Amendment

When the Manton amendment was added to the 1993 National Competitiveness Act, it fundamentally changed the dynamics of the foreign investment debate. The amendment pushed both performance requirements and CNT too far, too fast, provoking sharp criticism from American-owned multinationals concerned about threats to corporate flexibility.[18] The amendment thereby united American and foreign-owned firms into a formidable opposition force, prompting the first serious review of the conditional national treatment proposition and the use of foreign investors as a trade tool. An unexpected side benefit was also the new momentum generated toward multilateral negotiations on barriers to transnational investing though forums such as the Organization for Economic Cooperation and Development (OECD) and a WTO for investment.

The debate also caught the attention of the White House. Opposition from the Clinton administration helped to highlight the negative consequences from efforts like Manton to manage international investment flows. Secretary Ron Brown of the Commerce Department argued that the amendment's CNT provisions could hurt the economy and move the United States toward "the worst possible policy" by denying "the U.S. economy foreign know-how that would otherwise benefit economic growth and enhance U.S. productivity."[19]

Although the Clinton administration opposed CNT in the case of Manton, it has not—in contrast with past administrations—issued a firm statement renewing an unconditional U.S. commitment to an open-door policy based on the principles of national treatment and nondiscrimination.[20] Instead, in other cases, such as the proposed deregulation of the American financial service industry, the Clinton administration has endorsed conditional national treatment and the use of congressional mandates to open markets (see table A–1).

The debate over managed investment, as a result, is just getting started. The Manton amendment was simply the wake-up call. With the Uruguay Round completed, a GATT for investment is the next major area of both conflict and opportunity for expanding global markets. Differences in internal market policies will continue to generate both "system friction" and calls for aggressive forms of reciprocity, as policy entrepreneurs search for new tools to level the playing field and manage investment flows. The Manton amendment may be dead, but the pressure persists for U.S. legislators to link federal benefits and regulations in fields like telecommunications to the liberalization of trade and investment practices abroad. The absence of multilateral rules in many of these areas—such as eligibility conditions for public R&D programs—creates pernicious opportunities for mischief and special-interest appeals.

The challenge is to inform policy makers and their advisers, so that we do not lurch in a variety of directions and thereby increase business uncertainty and curtail economic opportunities. For starters, how should American economic interests be defined? Does it make economic sense to use foreign investors, especially in high-tech industries, as a crowbar to increase U.S. leverage in international negotiations? An even more fundamental question raised by the conditional national treatment proposition is whether the trade-off it involves between the promotion of inward foreign investment and the reduction of market barriers abroad makes sense. Is this trade-off necessary? And if it is, what are the costs and benefits of this approach?

In this volume key members of the policy and research communities examine these questions by focusing on two sets of issues:

• How do national treatment and an open door on foreign investment contribute to the U.S. economy? Conversely, what are the economic implications of the alternatives, such as the proposed use of foreign investors as a crowbar?

• On tactics, do we need Congress to get tough with our trading partners by mandating conditional national treatment and equivalent treatment standards? Should the mission of opening markets be attached to technology programs? Or are there more cost-effective options for reducing barriers to transnational investing?

The contributors to this volume draw on their practical experience as negotiators and policy advisers as well as on their work on the relationships between foreign direct investment and the economy. They include Richard Florida, professor of management and public policy at Carnegie Mellon University; Clyde V. Prestowitz, president of Economic Strategy Institute; Daniel M. Price, of Powell, Goldstein, Frazer & Murphy and former USTR negotiator on investment issues in NAFTA; and Ellen L. Frost, counselor at the Office of the U.S. Trade Representative.

Chapter 2 provides the background for the discussion with a brief history of the policy trends and an overview of the links between the continuing managed trade debate and the emerging debate over foreign investment. It also critically examines conditional national treatment as a senseless proposition that pits two worthwhile economic objectives against each other—namely, the promotion of inward foreign direct investment and the reduction of market access barriers (trade or investment) abroad. On tactics, the chapter concludes that the CNT approach manages to threaten the successful open door policy of the United States while doing little to advance broader American objectives in reducing foreign barriers to transnational investing.

Chapters 3 through 7 examine in more detail both the economic role of foreign direct investment and the never-ending search for more leverage in international negotiations. Although there is agreement among the contributors on the positive role that foreign investment has played in the development of the U.S. economy, opinions differ on the significance of this role and the direction U.S. investment policy should take in the years ahead.

Richard Florida argues in chapter 3 that congressional experiments with conditional national treatment are pulling the United States in the wrong direction—one that will undermine the dynamic capability of the U.S. economy. The open-door policies of the United States, he points out, have attracted the best companies from around the world. No other country or region has the same competitive advantage. As a result, the United States has "witnessed an economic miracle of sorts" in the transformation of the nation's rust belt into one of the world's leading export regions.

In chapter 4, Clyde Prestowitz argues that managed investment policies are needed when our trading partners play by different rules. He argues that in general, the unilateral free trade (open-door) position is insupportable because it does not ensure the best of all possible worlds. He takes issue with Florida's view that all foreign investment should be accepted as good for the economy. A more practical approach, he suggests, is for the United States to discriminate between investors based on the investment and market-access conditions in their home countries. Conditioning the national treatment of foreign investors, Prestowitz concludes, will give U.S. negotiators the necessary leverage to improve these market conditions.

Daniel Price and Ellen Frost argue respectively in chapters 5 and 6 that U.S. negotiators do not need CNT measures to gain leverage or to make progress in international negotiations. Both point to recent gains in these negotiations and elaborate on additional steps that must be taken toward multilateral investment rules. Price rejects Prestowitz's framing of the debate, as well as his conclusion. Although barriers clearly exist abroad, Price argues that the answer lies in negotiation, not heavy-handed congressional mandates. "The choice is not between unilateral free trade and intervention," in his view, but rather between tools for reducing discriminatory investment barriers. He charts a path for progressive liberalization of those barriers, concluding that the objective in these negotiations—the promotion of national treatment and foreign investment flows—should not be sacrificed to the search for more leverage.

Ellen Frost also takes issue with the proposition that reciprocity mandates are needed from Congress to address investment and market access barriers. She points to the power of existing tools, such as section 301, to gain leverage in international negotiations on market access, and to the potential for multilateral mechanisms to meet the longer-term need for basic rules on investment conditions. Chapter 7 concludes the policy discussion by looking at some of the obstacles in the path of multilateral rules.

Chapter 8 rounds out the discussion with a detailed review of the empirical literature on the role of foreign investment in the U.S. economy. Richard Florida finds that FDI and unhindered investment flows have been critical for U.S. economic growth. Europe, by contrast, tried to limit the role of foreign investors, and in the process it undercut the competitiveness of domestic firms in several key industries. Rather than imitate these mistakes, Florida concludes, the United States has to build on the tangible economic success of its own investment policy and to renew its commitment to an open door. Unlike conditional national treatment, he argues, this course is both practical and necessary.

Areas for Future Research

Changes in the world economy over the past decade have both challenged the open-door position of the United States and presented new opportunities for advancing its underlying principles at the multilateral level. Leaders in the business and research communities have a key role to play in informing the policy debate. The contributors to this volume have put forward a foundation on which to build, but much more remains to be done. Several areas stand out as particularly relevant for future research:

• **Trade and Investment.** Much of the conditional national treatment debate on investment assumes that trade follows outward flows of investment and that the lack of comparable investment opportunities abroad will therefore curtail export and jobs at home. Recent reports from the Office of Technology Assessment have further questioned the value of some types of inward FDI, because of the supporting flows of imports. The assumption is that outward investment is good and inward investment can be bad. This contrasts sharply with the view expressed in the mandated national benefits test, which uses inward investment in the United States as the appropriate base to define the value of a given firm to the economy, in various technology-policy programs. To set a more consistent course for policy, the links between trade and investment must therefore be clarified and the evidence integrated into the investment debate.

• **The Zero-Sum Proposition.** Proponents of managed-investment policies such as CNT often assume that differences in foreign-investment and internal-market policies between the United States and its trading partners detract from U.S. economic welfare. Under what conditions, if any, does this assumption hold? Alternatively, when is foreign investment in the United States a zero-sum game? In what industries? Are they the exception or the rule?

• **Market Access and FDI.** How should the relationship between market access and foreign direct investment be defined? What do theory and experience tell us about the ratio of foreign direct investment to GDP as an indicator of market access?

• **The Importance of Japan.** How important will FDI be in Japan over the next decade—especially in those industries listed by the U.S. government as critical? How important are the dynamic East Asian economies?

• **Liberalization and Investment Environment.** The internationalization of business and the increasing interdependence of international economies have faded the lines between domestic and foreign policies, exposing internal-market policies to a new level of international scrutiny. In this context, what is the difference between the liberalization of investment policies and the creation of an attractive investment climate? When are the policy differences across countries legitimate in creating an attractive investment climate? Which areas should be harmonized at the multilateral level?

- **International and Domestic Law.** What are the implications of the Uruguay Round and the continuing OECD discussions on a Multilateral Investment Agreement for U.S. domestic laws that affect foreign direct investment (section 301, special 301, and ATP)?
- **Services and FDI.** Almost any comparison between services and manufacturing produces a long list of differences between the two sectors. Given the importance of services, which account for more than 50 percent of international investment flows, what are the implications of these differences for the development of multilateral rules in investment? Will services and manufacturing require different sets of rules? Will industries within the service sector require different multilateral rules?
- **Financing FDI.** New data suggest that domestic capital plays a key role in the financing of foreign direct investments of both American and foreign-owned firms. Is this pattern unique to the United States? And what are the implications of global capital markets for FDI flows and policy?
- **FDI and Networked Firms.** How will the emergence of networked firms as business units, brought about through measures such as strategic alliances, change the role of FDI? What are the implications for investment and trade policies, based on the concept of bounded firms as opposed to a network of firms?

These are a sample of the questions that must be addressed for future policy discussions. What follows are the provocative analyses of the underlying themes that lay the necessary foundation for them.

2

Foreign Investors Make Lousy Crowbars

Cynthia A. Beltz

For most of its history the United States has maintained an open-door policy on foreign investment, based on the philosophy that it promotes domestic economic growth.[1] Even those hailed as visionary leaders by today's managed traders have pointed to the positive economic role that foreign investment plays in the economy. Alexander Hamilton, for example, argued in his *Report on Manufacturers* that foreign investment, "rather than be judged a rival, ought to be considered an auxiliary all the more precious because it permits an increased amount of productive labor and useful enterprise to be set to work."[2] On the free-trade side of the fence, the Reagan administration set forth U.S. policy as one that "provides foreign investors fair, equitable, and nondiscriminatory treatment under our laws and regulations."[3] As President George Bush put it, "unhindered international investment" is "beneficial to all nations; it is a positive-sum game."[4]

This open door on investment, unlike trade under the GATT, is not anchored by a single text but rather by a series of bilateral, regional, and multilateral agreements. In particular, U.S. treaties of Friendship, Commerce, and Navigation (FCNs) and more recently the Bilateral Investment Treaties (BITs) have promoted treatment of foreign investors that is no less favorable than that accorded domestic investors (national treatment) and the elimination of performance requirements as a condition of establishment and expansion.[5] The purpose is not only to protect the right of U.S. investors to be treated fairly around the world but also to build a body of practice supporting predictable and nondiscriminatory rules that will protect the rights of investors from all countries.

A major challenge to this objective, ironically, comes from the United States itself. A new generation of laws and propositions that has

16

gained ground in the past four years assumes that the unhindered access of foreign investors is a luxury the United States can no longer afford—especially when others do not play by our rules or when their economies are organized differently. Regulatory differences between countries, we are told, reduce comparable opportunities for American transnationals to invest abroad, curtail exports from the United States, and create "significant disadvantages" for the general "vitality of the U.S. economy." The argument continues that the United States must replace its open-door policy of national treatment with that of a managed gateway based on conditional national treatment, according to which the treatment of foreign investors would vary by country of origin and industry.[6]

The underlying notion is the familiar claim that the rest of the world is free riding at America's expense. Or, as Stephen Krasner of Stanford University has said, an open system guarantees the United States a "sucker's payoff" when other systems are only partially open. To level the playing field and promote U.S. economic interests, the CNT argument continues, the United States needs leverage in the shape of a tit-for-tat strategy—alternately referred to as specific reciprocity or conditional MFN (CMFN)—and the equivalent exchange of benefits.[7]

Similarly, others, such as the Economic Strategy Institute, have attacked America's open door on investment as a policy based on "ideological beliefs, not rational considerations."[8] For "national and economic security-related industries" (which seem to include most high-technology industries), a 1991 ESI report concluded in particular that the United States should manage investment actively, explore "U.S.-ownership solutions," and impose performance requirements on those foreign-owned firms that purchase key American companies. Additional restrictions on foreign investment were promoted in a 1993 ESI study on airlines. The report argues for the specific reciprocity principle—that is, foreign investment in an industry should be deferred until a bilateral treaty ensures an "equal exchange of opportunity" for U.S. investors in that industry.[9]

Two-Front Challenge

More disturbing than the reports and the rhetoric is the appeal of managed-investment ideas in Washington. Starting with the national security provision to restrict foreign acquisitions of American-owned firms, congressional experiments with managed investment and the conditioning of foreign investors have expanded in recent years to include commercial activities in a wide range of advanced technologies.

National and Economic Security Provisions. The Exon-Florio provision, passed in 1988, helped to establish for the first time in the United States a formal screening process for foreign investment. The provision gives the president the authority—without judicial review—to block a foreign-controlled firm's acquisition of an American firm if that acquisition threatens to impair national security. In the process, Exon-Florio sets up American-owned firms as the proxy for the national interest and foreign-owned firms as the strategic threat. The now-famous "Who is American?" question is thereby answered on the basis of corporate ownership.[10]

The power of Exon-Florio lies not in its actual application—the only takeover blocked to date occurred in 1990, when a Chinese firm was forced to divest its interest in a Seattle-based airplane-parts supplier. Instead, its power rests on the ownership standard it establishes and the legal authority it gives the government to restrict inward foreign investment in a potentially wide range of high-tech industries. Pressure exists, for example, to stretch the already elastic definition of *national security* to include protection of American-owned firms in those areas defined by some as vital to economic security or something vaguely termed as *U.S. competitiveness*.[11] Even without an explicit mandate to block acquisitions in these areas, the review process can discourage investment because of the uncertainty over how national security will be defined. This problem will only get worse as the United States moves toward a dual-use strategy to develop both traditional military and commercial industries. Exon-Florio, as a result, has the potential to be a significant anti-FDI device in industries that are primarily commercial in nature.[12]

The review process has further encouraged the use of foreign investors in the United States as a trade tool. In 1986, for example, the Japanese firm Fujitsu sought an 80 percent interest in the American firm Fairchild Semiconductor Corporation. Although Fairchild was already owned by a foreign company (Schlumberger of France), the United States wanted to get tough on trade with Japan. The national security review and the Fujitsu bid accordingly became a bargaining chip in the maneuvering of American officials trying to open Japanese markets. Fujitsu eventually dropped its bid.[13]

The pernicious power of the Fairchild case lies in what the U.S.

government did not do. It did not restrict FDI outright as a general rule and thereby gain a reputation as a protectionist, but instead manipulated the regulatory process to discriminate against a foreign firm. This was all done in an effort to gain negotiating leverage—a tactic with considerable political appeal. In the late 1980s after the Fairchild case, for example, a series of bills were introduced that linked the treatment of foreign investors in U.S. sectors such as cable television and financial services to the willingness of their home-country governments to give comparable access to their markets.[14] The call was for restrictions abroad to be matched by equivalent restrictions at home.

Technology Policy. In the 1990s the legal framework for treating foreign-owned firms as bargaining chips has been advanced through federal R&D programs for the commercial sector and the high-tech community. Under the umbrella of these programs, the federal government now has expanded its authority (outside of national security) to discriminate against foreign investors and to penalize them for the practices of their home-country governments. Proponents do not advertise the strategy as anti–foreign investment, but rather as pro–"fair" trade and investment conditions. The policy also is not portrayed as favoring discriminatory investment rules but rather as garnering leverage for U.S. negotiators to open markets abroad. Irrespective of the spin, however, the effect of CNT is the same—the promotion of investment discrimination in the United States.

Take, for example, the precedent set by the Advanced Technology Program (ATP) in the Department of Commerce, which was the cornerstone of President Clinton's high-tech plan. Under ATP, before a foreign-owned firm can get the same treatment as its American counterpart, it first must pass a qualifying test by demonstrating that its home-country government provides "adequate and effective" protection of intellectual property rights (IPR) as well as local investment opportunities and "comparable" access to R&D programs for American multinationals. Under current law, as a result of the CNT tests, a foreign company may be held responsible for the practices of its home government even in areas not directly related to investment or to the sector in which the company is active in the United States.

Like an undetected computer virus, the ATP conditional national treatment language has spread to four other laws dealing with the high-tech sector as well as to twelve proposals in areas ranging from financial services to R&D in environment and aerospace technolo-

19

gies (see table A–1). As Dan Price argues in chapter 5, there is no natural limit to how far the CNT virus can spread. Academic proponents of CNT are already on the move, advocating that "the preferences built into federal R&D programs be used as part of a broad trade strategy, insisting on reciprocity to increase access to foreign markets and know-how."[15] Proposed policy tools include not only manipulating the access to American technology programs but also the discriminatory treatment of foreign multinationals under U.S. tax policy and other areas of federal regulation.

Specific reciprocity measures are already the latest rage in Washington. Disputes over financial services, airlines, and telecommunications have produced legislation and policy initiatives to link deregulation and the removal of remaining ownership restrictions in the United States to the liberalization of markets abroad. In telecommunications, for example, the United States is aggressively pushing bilateral reciprocity (as defined by the United States) with its G-7 trading partners. The demand is for "effective market access" before American telecommunications services will be opened—by a new law or regulation—to foreign investors. This shift toward aggressive reciprocity is a particularly disturbing development, in that services account for a growing share of FDI flows (more than 45 percent in 1993).

Removing America's Doorstop

The fundamental issue raised by the CNT movement, therefore, is whether Congress should get into the business of using foreign investors as a crowbar to advance U.S. international trade and investment objectives. Is this the precedent the United States wants to set for other countries, especially dynamic developing economies, to follow?

There are two major reasons to reject this proposition. First, it does not make economic sense. The evidence does not support the underlying "sucker's payoff" thesis—namely, that an open door on FDI has disadvantaged the American economy. Further, on tactics, the CNT approach is unsatisfying because it threatens the benefits gained from an open-door policy while doing little to advance broader American objectives in opening markets abroad. It discounts both the dynamic role that foreign investors play in the American economy and the myriad domestic and international problems created by implementing such a strategy.

A Choice in Tactics. The foreign investment debate is not about whether barriers to transnational investment exist. Clearly they do. Nor does the debate question American negotiating objectives— namely, the reduction of these barriers. Clearly, the United States must actively promote investment liberalization, both to increase trade and investment flows and to maintain the viability of its open-door policy. To be sustainable, such a policy must be both economically sound *and* politically viable. This requires a sense of balance and fairness. Or, as Irwin Stelzer of the American Enterprise Institute has written, "No litany of economic facts and data can sustain a policy that is widely seen as producing unfair results."[16] Efforts to balance benefits, as a result, have had a long history in the United States.

In trade, the United States initially took an aggressive bilateral approach to balancing benefits. Starting with the first commercial trade treaty signed with France in 1778, the United States linked access to the domestic market to access for U.S. products abroad. But the nature of this linkage has changed over time, from a focus on bilateral reciprocity to the adoption of unconditional MFN in the 1920s and the organization of the GATT in 1947.[17] The GATT replaced an array of reciprocal bilateral trade agreements with a broader approach to liberalization, based on a rough balancing of concessions at the multilateral level. These concessions are then generalized to all partners under MFN, with retaliation permitted in a measured form when the agreed-upon trade rules are broken. The GATT therefore emphasizes reciprocity in the fundamental sense that when a member country takes on obligations it receives the advantages (rights) that result from the obligations of others.[18]

In contrast to trade, the United States has consistently taken an approach to investment liberalization based on the principles of nondiscrimination. It has promoted binding rules and investment liberalization through negotiations (rather than unilateral determination of offensive practices) and the mutual definition of investor rights and legal obligations. These principles were not sacrificed at home in order to promote them abroad. Instead, the United States maintained its open door and used measures such as the FCNs and BITs to expand international commitments to basic investor rights. Under these agreements the United States concedes its inherent right to discriminatory (CMFN or CNT) policies, thereby taking on the legal obligation not to retreat from its open door. In return, it gains the

21

commitment of partner countries to national treatment or MFN, whichever is more advantageous, except in those areas listed and justified. The United States does not, however, match these exceptions on a case-by-case—or a specific reciprocity—basis. In the process, the United States improves the transparency of FDI restrictions and liberalization takes place as countries—especially developing countries—take on significant international obligations to forgo the use of many FDI restrictions.

The history of U.S. investment policy thus stands in sharp contrast with trade strategies aimed at leveling the playing field for specific industries through conditional MFN clauses or tit-for-tat tools such as section 301 of the 1974 Trade Act.[19] At times the United States has contemplated the use of trade barriers under section 301 to retaliate against unfair foreign-investment practices abroad, but it has not done so. Nor has it used retaliatory investment measures such as a denial of a regulatory license to a firm from the offending country.[20]

At its root, then, the conditional national treatment proposition is a choice about tactics for opening markets abroad. It is a choice that pits the aggressive reciprocity tactics advocated by managed trade proponents against the success and history of U.S. investment policy.[21]

Managed Trade and Investment. The similarities between the managed-trade and the current managed-investment movements are all too striking. Both are part of a congressional move to reassert its own constitutional authority in matters of foreign commerce. Both are motivated by the "fairness" doctrine and a search for the elusive level playing field at the bilateral and sectoral levels. Both also share a focus on results (effective national treatment) over rules (legal obligations). As two legal experts have written, "conditional national treatment substitutes specific results, demanded by Congress, for treaty norms. Thus it devalues treaties, including those beneficial to U.S.-owned businesses." [22] Further, instead of the "you help me, and I'll help you" form of reciprocity associated with the GATT, the CNT approach is closer to the "unless you help me, I'll hurt you" form of reciprocity associated with super 301.[23] This form of reciprocity has thus come explicitly to encompass protectionist moves or to open the door to the creation of new barriers.

Given the long-term goal of multilateral investment rules, the conditional national treatment focus on bilateral relationships is particularly troubling. The national treatment and MFN principles, in contrast, prohibit many forms of geographic discrimination and thereby promote a broader approach to liberalization and dispute settlement. Indeed, trade historians argue that GATT emphasizes the principle of MFN because "it is the engine of substantive multilateralism."[24] Presumably this is still the goal of U.S. investment policy as well, but the lessons of trade and GATT have been largely ignored by those pushing discriminatory investment measures or CMFN-based policies.

Another troubling dimension is the focus on unilateral definitions of reciprocity, or fair treatment. Instead of promoting multilateral or regional mechanisms to set international standards and settle disputes, CNT promotes the judge-and-jury roles played by the United States under Super 301. The CNT provisions try to push foreign governments beyond their GATT legal obligations to impose what the United States has defined as the appropriate standard in areas such as eligibility conditions for R&D programs. Under the precedent set by the ATP program, the United States would identify which foreign practices justify discriminatory treatment of investors, would mandate that the foreign government change the behavior, and would then unilaterally determine when the results are acceptable and the reciprocity conditions have been fulfilled. Yesterday's crowbar for adding force to demands of this type included trade sanctions under section 301 of the trade law. Tomorrow's crowbar may, if the notion of CNT is accepted, be foreign investors in the United States.

An Irrational and Impractical Policy

If the objective is to open markets abroad while doing little economic damage at home, then foreign investors—especially those in the high-tech sector—make the worst possible choice for a crowbar. The premise is that foreign investment in the United States should be restricted or only encouraged to the extent that it is permitted overseas. But such neomercantilist or zero-sum logic makes little sense in today's interconnected world economy, in which the importance of FDI is even more important than it was in years past—for firms and nations alike.

When investors in the United States are used as a crowbar, we will hurt ourselves more than anyone else. The discriminatory treatment of foreign investors in the United States directly affects, for example, their American workers, suppliers, communities, and domestic corporate partners. Any negative impact only trickles back indirectly to the government of the parent firm—not exactly a cost-effective technique either to garner leverage in international negotiations or to promote economic growth at home. Instead, if we let the policies of our trading partners determine our economic interests and negotiating tactics, we will "make the folly of others the limit of our wisdom."[25]

Discounting the Productivity Payoff. Part of the problem is perception. All too often in Washington, foreign investors are viewed as political pawns or a source of leverage. Elsewhere, workers, researchers, and their communities have experienced firsthand the value of foreign investment. Economic historians add further perspective, concluding that the openness of the United States to foreign capital has been "pivotal" and "central" to this country's economic development.[26] Yet proponents of CNT discount these benefits of FDI (actual and potential) even as its practical value is rising in the economy.

Consider the consumer electronics industry. Foreign-owned firms purchased American television firms in the late 1970s. Since then they have played a vital role in the development of new products, such as digital and interactive television, helping to make the United States the world leader in several advanced technologies.[27] As economist Rachel McCulloch has argued, it is precisely when inward direct investment is "a threat to domestic competitors that it is most likely to be a source of future strength for the economy as a whole."[28]

It is this dynamic role that is key for the economy, but is so often overlooked in the political debate. Yet the evidence is even more tangible today than in years past. Dramatic changes in FDI flows and business strategies over the past decade have put foreign and American-owned firms into direct competition, forcing them continually to upgrade and to match the best global practices. In the process, they have helped to improve productivity and U.S. economic welfare. As a result, far from the "sucker's payoff" claimed by critics, America's open door on investment has generated a productivity payoff.

A 1993 McKinsey Global Institute study found that FDI in the United States has played a powerful role in raising domestic productivity by increasing head-to-head competition with the best firms in the world. Those industries with less exposure to FDI and trade, in contrast, were productivity followers rather than leaders[29] (see figure A–6). A 1993 report from the Department of Commerce also concluded that foreign-owned firms "have contributed significantly to U.S. technological development." Instead of getting stuck with a lopsided bargain or naively hosting the free ride of foreign firms, the United States has gained from "an overwhelmingly large *net* inflow of technology to U.S. affiliates from their foreign parents," according to the study.[30]

In the process, foreign investors have helped to transform the nation's rust belt into an export belt, while providing "good" jobs for American workers. Research on the Great Lakes region demonstrates that far from hollowing out the industrial base—as critics have claimed—foreign direct investment has helped to turn the region into a world leader in the export of high value–added manufacturing goods, has boosted exports to twice the national average, and has thereby helped to make the United States once again the largest exporter in the world (see chapter 8). Equally misguided is the assumption that foreign-owned firms import only low-paying jobs while keeping the high-skill, high-wage jobs at home. A 1992 report of the Federal Reserve Bank of St. Louis concluded that there was no evidence to support this "screwdriver assembly" hypothesis, and reports from the Department of Commerce suggest that foreign-owned firms on average pay higher wages than do U.S.-owned firms.[31]

Foreign investors are therefore essential for updating and diversifying the technology base of the United States. With advanced technologies and the skills needed to harness them often globally dispersed, a vice president at IBM recently noted, "No single country is able to be the best at all critical technologies and skills at the same time." Governments that discourage inward FDI in these areas under the guise of opening markets abroad or promoting growth at home, therefore, do so at their own expense. Such measures undercut the competitiveness of companies, slow the application of technology, and ultimately disadvantage their citizens.[32]

Critics of America's open-door policy on investment do concede that foreign investment can play a positive role in the economy. But they nonetheless argue that CNT and CMFN make more economic sense than an unmanaged gateway, because not all investment is equally good for the economy. Presumably this concern could apply to both foreign and domestic investment. It is therefore not clear why the nationality of ownership should matter in this respect. Further, such critics assume that the use of foreign investors as a trade tool—whether through technology programs or other means—will ultimately generate more benefit for the domestic economy than would a policy of unhindered access.

Some types of investment (foreign or domestic) are undoubtedly better than others for the economy. But the government is poorly equipped to determine which types are best. An even more fundamental problem is the definition of *good* that prevails when a foreign-owned firm's treatment is linked, especially through the legislative process, to the practices of the home-country government. The United States has had an open door not simply as a matter of principle, but because it makes economic sense. Any standard other than one based on national treatment and MFN invites arbitrary and economically inconsistent interpretations.

For starters, CNT restrictions conflict with the dynamics of the global markets. They raise the risks involved in linking arms with a foreign-owned firm and thereby discourage what may otherwise be the beneficial participation of foreign-owned firms in areas like telecommunications or federal programs like ATP. To the extent that such measures are enforced, the United States will voluntarily curtail its ability to create a world-class technology base. Second, the definition of what is good for the economy should not be defined by the politics of reciprocity or the prevailing U.S. view on the "fairness" of the home country's government. If the government is going to develop a "good" investment standard to measure the merit of a firm's investment, it would be better to base it on the firm's economic contribution to the American economy. The peculiar CNT standard of a good investment undercuts the stated goals of our own technology programs and restricts American access to foreign technology even as we are pushing for increased access in international negotiations. This is economic nonsense, and it should be rejected.

Administrative Nightmares. The implementation of a policy based on CNT is also fraught with practical and political problems. The enforcement of congressional mandates on fair investment conditions would be a procedural nightmare. There is no easy set of guidelines. Rather, the federal investment police—those charged with checking out the program eligibility of foreign-owned firms—will confront a baffling array of international alliances as well as a series of "comparable" treatment definitions that will vary by country and industry. Some have already noted that federal agencies and courts seem free to apply inconsistent interpretations of congressionally mandated conditions of national treatment—for example, whether intellectual property is protected "effectively" in Country X—or to reach incon-

26

sistent results. Many of the administrators of the federal programs have further indicated they would prefer not to deal with such restrictions because of the difficulty of defining an American firm and the procedural problems that impede their R&D missions.[33]

To the extent that CNT mandates are enforced and tilt the playing field against a local producer, the investment police will also provoke a confrontation with the states. Discriminating against foreign-owned companies translates into discrimination against their 5 million employees, as well as the employees of their suppliers working in different states across the country. Indeed, the discounting of FDI reflected in the CNT initiatives reveals a disturbing disconnect between the states and Washington, where foreign investors do not seem to be valued as vehicles for economic development.

In theory, conditional national treatment and specific reciprocity could be used "prudently and conservatively," as advocates suggest.[34] Yet in practice, the review process that would have to be set up to administer the CNT tests ordered by Congress would more likely be used as a weapon to serve parochial interests. A statutory prohibition against FDI is not necessary to discourage what may otherwise be a useful contribution of FDI to the domestic economy. The case of the ATP program again makes the point. Under current law, even if a foreign-owned firm passes the national-benefits test required for all firms applying for an ATP grant, it would still have to pass a second, or a CNT, review that includes a specific reciprocity test (of the home country's local investment opportunities) and a fair-treatment test (on intellectual property). This review process leaves the firm vulnerable to harassment by a domestic rival. The potential for abuse has already been demonstrated, first by the Fujitsu case and then by the Exon-Florio review process. In *Regulation,* Susan Liebeler and William Lash report that the Exon-Florio review process is listed in securities law textbooks as a valid defense or delaying tactic against corporate takeovers that has already been tried more than 800 times. By contrast, from 1975 to 1988, only 30 cases had been reviewed for national security reasons under the Committee on Foreign Investment in the United States (CFIUS), which lacked enforcement authority until the Exon-Florio provision was passed in 1988.[35]

A Cracked Crowbar. Aside from the economic arguments against using foreign investors as a trade tool, the strategy does not fit the mission of promoting investment liberalization and the development of stable, predictable rules. Instead, it increases uncertainty by inviting our trading partners to retaliate with new investment barriers of their own. The United States is not the only country with hostages, and our relative bargaining power will accordingly be reduced to the extent that others can harass or retaliate against American transnational corporations.[36] On this point the United States is particularly vulnerable, as the leading supplier of foreign direct investment and as the home base for roughly 3,000 transnational corporations that account for 25 percent of total global outflows.[37]

Indeed, an inherent flaw of the CNT strategy is the strong incentive it creates for foreign governments to build negotiating leverage by retaliating with similar measures. By claiming the right to make unilateral decisions, the United States concedes the same right to others to determine what constitutes fair and reciprocal treatment of transnational firms. We had better be prepared for their response. They may imitate us, as they did in setting up antidumping laws. American firms are now often the target of these "unfair" laws. Discriminatory investment measures likewise could lead to "a legislative cross-fire inconsistent with today's global economy,"[38] curtailing rather than enhancing the access of American-owned transnationals to foreign markets and research programs. What may thus appear to help in the short term would work instead to reduce corporate flexibility and constrain the efficiency of global operations over the longer term.

The CNT approach is further prone to failure as a negotiating tactic because of the nature of many of the FDI barriers involved. In the case of developing countries, few have transnational firms operating in the United States, leaving our government few hostages to use as bargaining chips. In the case of industrialized countries, many of the investment barriers facing transnational firms are structural in nature, or there is no clear consensus on the appropriate international standard or on how it should be implemented. Regarding Japan, for example, there is widespread agreement that many of the major barriers to FDI are private and structural and therefore by definition difficult for the government to change.[39] It is also difficult to ascertain what constitutes "comparable" or "fair" treatment in many areas outside the GATT but linked to traditional investing. Even the United States would have difficulty passing some of the reciprocity tests suggested by Congress. Take, for example, the test on standards proposed under the Manton amendment. The Department of Commerce has said that the United States might not pass the "open and transparent" test because many American private–sector standards organizations do not allow foreign participation or membership.[40]

The United States should also learn from its own experience in trade policy on the practical deficiencies of specific reciprocity. Or as Robert Keohane of Harvard University has said, serious doubt exists about "whether the evidence from trade negotiations supports the proposition that specific reciprocity facilitates international negotiation."[41] From 1778 until the 1930s, most commercial treaties included a CMFN clause, and the United States extended tariff concessions on the condition that the other country pay for them with equivalent concessions or compensation. The United States was the only country that insisted on using a CMFN clause, making it the free rider. Meanwhile, the United States benefited from the concessions granted under the MFN-based policies of other countries without giving anything in return. The strategy was intended to promote international agreements by extending benefits on a quid pro quo basis, such that any market-opening move made by the United States would be extended to another country only if that country provided "equivalent" compensation to the United States. Nice idea, but the strategy failed.

It failed because specific reciprocity worked better in theory than in practice, for several reasons: *equivalent* was often too difficult to define; the temptation to erect barriers for bargaining purposes was significant; and negotiators grew concerned that the policy would, at best, result in an infinite series of bilateral bargains to be negotiated. U.S. Assistant Secretary of State Frances Bowes Sayre concluded that CMFN "is manifestly impractical and unsatisfactory. It involves unceasing and difficult negotiations which are quite unnecessary and costly."[42] U.S. Tariff Commissioner W.S. Culbertson wrote that CMFN "has hindered more than it has helped the development of our foreign trade."[43] Secretary of State Charles Evans Hughes added that "the United States needs a guarantee of equality of treatment which cannot be furnished by the conditional form of the most-favored nation clause."[44] Jacob Viner described the CMFN clause as the cause of "international ill feeling, conflict between international obligations and municipal law" and "confusion and uncertainty of operations."[45] Further, whatever benefits may have been gained on an individual-case basis were quickly overwhelmed by the administrative costs of a policy that treated firms differently even if they were in the same product area or industry.

As a result of these problems, the United States reversed direction in 1923 and exchanged its insistence on CMFN for an unconditional MFN clause. MFN does not require the specific reciprocity bilateral balancing act, and it limits geographic discrimination through the extension of trade concessions to any other country with which the United States has a trade agreement. The United States further incorporated MFN into the Trade Agreements Act of 1934, helped to make it a founding principle of the GATT in 1947, and in the process helped to institute nondiscrimination as a guiding principle for the multilateral system of rules on international trade.

U.S. trade history—replete with experiments and institutional innovations of the GATT—thus has many lessons for the current debate over investment policy. Many of the ideas now gaining popularity, such as specific reciprocity, have already been tried and rejected. As Robert Keohane has said, "The failure of the conditional MFN clause should make us cautious about specific reciprocity. . . . In complex multilateral situations perhaps involving domestic politics as well as international relations, its results may frustrate those who seek stable, beneficial agreements."[46] Unless the long-term goal of U.S. investment policy has changed, the United States therefore has even more reason to reject the specific-reciprocity proposition as it turns to the task of shaping a WTO for investment in a world that grows ever more complicated and contentious.

Looking Ahead

Barriers to transnational investing do exist, of course. But, an American retreat from an open-door policy toward congressional mandates and CNT experiments contributes to the problem, not the solution. Not only is such a policy schizophrenic in nature, applying one standard to the United States and another to foreign countries; it also conflicts with long-term U.S. objectives to promote technological developments, domestic economic growth, and a stable system of nondiscriminatory investment rules that protect the rights of investors from all countries.

Ultimately we will need some form of multilateral framework such as a WTO for investment. The framework would have to be strong and broad enough to attract the participation of the major FDI supplier and host countries. The practical value of accepted and uniform rules is the objective standard they provide for governments to judge each other, thereby curtailing the role of power politics or "rule of the jungle." The practical problem, of course, is the age-old challenge to national sovereignty that has delayed a GATT-for-investment for nearly fifty years and that almost blocked U.S. acceptance of the World Trade Organization in 1994. How to get from here to such multilateral rules thus is a major challenge confronting the United States today.

Even by trade standards, the development of a multilateral framework on investment has been particularly uneven. Such an agreement on global investment principles was discussed in 1947 as part of the draft Havana Charter, but it failed to gain approval.[47] In the 1960s and 1970s, renewed efforts were made to create a systematic framework through bilateral investment treaties (BITs) as well as regional and multilateral negotiations. But the turning point may ultimately prove to be the unilateral liberalization movement among recent developing countries and the possibility that now exists for widespread interest in a framework of basic multilateral rules.

Progress toward these rules involves two related paths: establishing rules on official foreign direct investment barriers and establishing competition policy rules that address structural or private practices. Advancing down the second path will be a long and tedious journey, because there is little agreement on substantive standards for competition policy. Differences exist not only between nations but also within nations as to the appropriate standards for competition policy. The prospects for progress on the first path are more promising. The desire for investment reform is growing, and there is already substantive agreement on the major elements: right of establishment; national treatment; elimination of performance requirements; investment protection measures on intellectual property and corporate transfers (repatriation of profits); and a multilateral settlement mechanism for state-to-state as well as investor-to-state disputes.[48] For the major forums discussing these standards and member countries, see figure 2–1.

The Uruguay Round. The Uruguay Round helped to lay some of the necessary groundwork by applying GATT rules at the multilateral level for the first time to those areas of investment that have a direct impact on trade. The TRIMs prohibit local content requirements. The General Agreement on Trade in Services (GATS) provides a starting point for a multilateral FDI regime in the service sector, which accounts for more than 50 percent of global FDI flows. The agreement on trade-related aspects of intellectual property rights (TRIP) further provides a minimum standard of investment protection by

31

FIGURE 2–1
FORUMS ON INTERNATIONAL INVESTMENT RULES

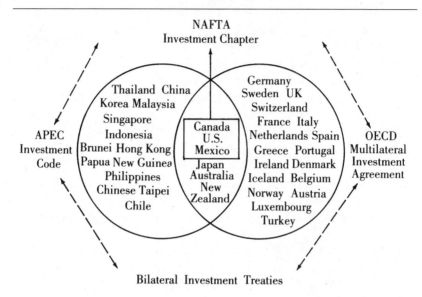

NAFTA
Investment Chapter

APEC
Investment
Code

Thailand China
Korea Malaysia
Singapore
Indonesia
Brunei Hong Kong
Papua New Guinea
Philippines
Chinese Taipei
Chile

Canada
U.S.
Mexico
Japan
Australia
New
Zealand

Germany
Sweden UK
Switzerland
France Italy
Netherlands Spain
Greece Portugal
Ireland Denmark
Iceland Belgium
Norway Austria
Luxembourg
Turkey

OECD
Multilateral
Investment
Agreement

Bilateral Investment Treaties

SOURCE: Based on Douglas C. Worth, Statement of Chairman of the OECD
Business and Industry Trade Advisory Committee, July 1994.

requiring compliance with major international conventions (World
Intellectual Property Organization, Paris and Berne).[49] On the issue
of standards, which in part motivated the CNT language in the Manton amendment, business groups and the Clinton administration have
concluded that "the progress made in the Uruguay Round and the
new enforcement mechanism of the World Trade Organization
promise to remove many of the barriers caused by problems such as
nonrecognition of testing results and lack of participation in standards development."[50]

Outside the GATT. Beyond the GATT, activity is already on the
rise in a variety of bilateral, regional, and multilateral forums aimed
at setting international standards for entry conditions, ownership,
and transfer of technology, as well as dispute settlements.

At the bilateral level, as of October 1994, more than 600 investment treaties have been signed by OECD countries—a 50 percent

increase from the 400 signed at the beginning of 1992.[51] These treaties have provided, especially in the absence of a broader mechanism, a useful starting point for reducing barriers. But the BITs are an inadequate substitute for a transparent and comprehensive investment code. The rules in BITs are often inconsistent across countries and sectors. Even within the U.S. system of thirty-four BITs, the language varies. The resulting patchwork and uncertainty contrasts with the more uniform system of predictable trade rules under the GATT.

The NAFTA investment chapter represents the first major step toward a comprehensive code. It is based on a broad commitment to national treatment. It covers measures imposed at the federal, state, and local levels. It addresses all aspects of investment operations (entry, establishment, and protection of foreign affiliates). It prohibits, for example, performance requirements on establishment, such as local content and domestic purchasing requirements. Also addressed were factors that affect business decisions after establishment, such as standards on intellectual property, antitrust enforcement, R&D, and tax treatment.[52] NAFTA further provides an important model for shaping a multilateral investment-dispute mechanism.

The next step may come as a result of the discussions in the Organization for Economic Cooperation and Development (OECD), which provides a unique forum for advancing policy discussions in areas like investment, which cut across a range of issues only partly covered by GATT. The OECD's discussions on the Multilateral Investment Agreement (formerly known as the Wider Investment Instrument), begun in 1991, could serve as a platform for broader agreement under the WTO. Thus far, the discussions have focused on developing a framework among "like-minded" countries for extending the investment disciplines of the BITs to the multilateral level. Of particular interest is the opportunity (under a working group chaired by the United States) for the development of a multilateral mechanism to resolve disputes between investors and the host country. The other working groups include those on existing liberalization, new liberalization disciplines (competition and subsidy policies), investment protection, and involvement of nonmembers.

The continuing nonbinding discussions through the forum on Asian Pacific Economic Cooperation (APEC), begun in 1989 by eighteen Pacific Rim countries, may also advance the development of multilateral investment standards.[53] (For a list of OECD and APEC members, see figure 2–1.) By participating in both forums

(OECD and APEC), the United States serves as a bridge and also as a catalyst. Competition between the two forums creates, for example, an interesting dynamic that may facilitate acceptance of a strong multilateral standard for cross-border flows of investment. Fear of exclusion and of being left behind can be powerful incentives for action. U.S. negotiators, however, will have their hands full over the next several years in channeling this energy and shaping the various agendas stirred up in 1994 to achieve strong investment rules.

Meanwhile, the private sector is not waiting for U.S. negotiators to overcome their obstacles to market access. Once again, standards provide a case in point. The American National Standards Institute (ANSI) worked successfully with the European standards-setting organizations to resolve the majority of issues raised by U.S. industry.[54]

Finally, the market itself is providing a powerful source of pressure for investment liberalization—especially in developing countries. Traditional anxiety over transnational corporations is being offset by a growing concern within these countries that they are being excluded from the globalization process and its accompanying benefits. During the global surge in FDI flows in the 1980s, for example, developing countries attracted only 21 percent of the total. Competition for foreign investment in the 1990s drove developing countries to liberalize their FDI policies, with more than forty countries doing so in 1992 alone. The developing-country share of global FDI flows is now on the rise and reached 32 percent in 1992. The drive toward reform is expected to continue as countries search for measures to raise average returns on investment. The United Nations even speculates that as a result of these liberalization trends, returns on investment in developing countries will approach 25 percent, while those for developed countries dip toward 15 percent.[55] The rise in competition for investment funds is further suggested by a 1994 Harris poll, which found that 75 percent of leading European business executives believe that China and Southeast Asian countries will offer the best manufacturing investment opportunities over the next fifteen years.[56]

Whether from developing countries (such as China, Malaysia, Mexico, and Argentina) or from its OECD trading partners, the United States will face increased competition for the investments of transnational firms in the decade ahead. In this world, initiatives that treat foreign-owned firms more as political pawns than as valued economic players are doomed to fail. To compete effectively, the United States needs a consistent policy framework that promotes both inward and outward investment flows. Ownership-based definitions of American interests (in public R&D programs or the shaping of an investment liberalization strategy) are simply too narrow to handle the world of complex interdependence growing up around transnational corporations. As one business executive recently commented, "policy must be reshaped to fit the world as it is becoming, not as it was."[57] Clearly much work remains to be done.

Members of Congress and the administration will have to resist pressures to weaken investment disciplines at home. Conditional national treatment may be politically appealing, but "the national treatment doctrine exists," as one legal expert recently commented, "because alternative approaches inevitably succumb to arbitrary, inconsistent, and locally biased interpretation. Conditional national treatment is not national treatment at all. It is an oxymoron."[58] Instead of experimenting with this approach, the United States has to renew its commitment to national treatment and MFN at home while building on NAFTA and the trends toward liberalization in the developing countries to make the case for comprehensive investment rules at the multilateral level. In the meantime, as needed, the United States should use existing investment treaties more aggressively to negate the portrayal of the United States as a "patsy" and thereby to limit the political appeal of CNT initiatives.[59]

Throughout the process, members of the business and academic communities must educate members of the policy community on the benefits and challenges of transnational investing. A key challenge will be to design and highlight alternatives to conditional national treatment measures for opening foreign markets to American investors, especially in the conflict-ridden industries of financial services, airlines, and telecommunications. More than any set of CNT initiatives, these steps will help to provide the experience, strategic framework, and forward-looking policies necessary to confront the economic and market access struggles effectively in the decade ahead. To prosper, the U.S. economy will increasingly rely on foreign investment and the competition it encourages. It is not something to take for granted or gamble lightly with in congressional or international negotiations.

3

Conditioning Investment Is a Losing Strategy

Richard Florida

International investment flows are the key to growth for both the domestic and the global economies. The problem is that the climate for investment in the United States and for R&D partnerships internationally may be getting worse. The chief officer for technology strategy at a major European multinational recently said that American firms are wary of entering partnerships with his company because the Americans risk being denied a federal contract by being linked with a German firm. In fact, he added, the legal obstacles to investing or participating in R&D joint ventures are greater in the United States than in Japan. Clearly, our nation must take a step back and carefully consider what is happening to U.S. investment policy.

In the United States we used to treat all companies equally. But Congress is now drifting toward a policy of treating companies differently based on their nationalities—conditional national treatment (CNT). The standard is not based on the worth of the company, but on the practices of the company's home country. A company from a "bad" country may get penalized. This is a bad strategy for the American economy. We should be encouraging, not discouraging, foreign investment. The United States has benefited disproportionately from the explosion in international investment. A key advantage has been our ability to attract international investment and to provide a climate where transplant companies are welcome, jobs are created, productivity is enhanced, and the industrial base is transformed.

Attracting the Best and the Brightest

Both Japan and Europe have great companies, but only the United States has the best Japanese, European, and U.S. companies in the same place.

That translates into a tremendous performance advantage for the twenty-first century. International investors account for one-fourth of all U.S. exports (roughly $100 billion) each year. Japanese companies in Japan say they would love to attract Western researchers, but it is very difficult to get them to relocate permanently to Japan. Before a country can harness the world's best brainpower, it is necessary for companies to invest in that country's economy. The great competitive advantage the United States has over Japan is that we can attract that brainpower.

Consider the returns in terms of productivity growth. The ability of the United States to attract international investment has been critical to the sweeping economic transformation and improvements in productivity growth that the United States has achieved over the past decade. U.S. productivity growth has outdistanced that of its major rivals in the advanced industrialized countries. International investment is the key to this growth. Recent studies by the McKenzie Global Institute[1] and the Organization for Economic Cooperation and Development (OECD)[2] show conclusively that international investment stimulates productivity, employment, and economic growth. The U.S. experience demonstrates that offshore manufacturing facilities, or transplants, play a particularly important role. In the United States, foreign-owned manufacturing companies have higher productivity rates and invest more in plant and equipment than U.S.-owned manufacturers, for example. (For details see the productivity section in chapter 8, and figure A–5.)

Transplants and the Technology Base

Transplant manufacturers also play a key role in developing the U.S. technology base. They transfer to the domestic economy state-of-the-art technology and such state-of-the-art business practices as total quality management, team-based work organization, the involvement of supplier in the innovation process, and the involvement of workers in productivity- and performance-improving measures. Fifteen percent of the total U.S. R&D base comes from foreign affiliates. Data that I compiled on the global R&D laboratories in the United States show nearly 400 international R&D units in the United States that together spend more than $11 billion per year on R&D.[3] (See the R&D and technology section in chapter 8, and figure A–7.)

Foreign investment, according to the OECD, is also good for employment, creating new jobs at a faster rate than domestic investment does in ten of the fifteen advanced industrial nations studied. In the United States, foreign investment has generated nearly 5 million jobs for American workers, with employment concentrated in the technology-intensive and high-wage manufacturing sectors. (See the employment and jobs section in chapter 8, and figure A–12.)

The Transforming Power of Japanese Investment

Some critics of an open investment environment have singled out Japan as a unique case that perhaps deserves special attention from the U.S. government. It is important to note, however, that over the past decade, 1,000 Japanese manufacturing plants have been established in the United States. Automotive-related sectors are home to 500 of these plants, which brought $26 billion in investment and created 110,000 direct manufacturing jobs. Contrary to the stereotype of these plants as screwdriver assembly plants, they have played a powerful role in transforming how American managers view production organization and labor-management relations, helping managers to harness workers' minds as well as their hands. (See the transplants section in chapter 8, and table A–4.)

Research also shows that, contrary to popular belief, Japanese companies do not avoid unions. An economic analysis of the location decisions of more than 450 Japanese-owned automotive-related establishments conducted in collaboration with Donald Smith of the RAND Institute has shown conclusively that these companies locate themselves in urban areas with high union concentrations. The key to their location decisions is being close to a hub assembly facility that they supply.[4]

Japanese steel makers have also invested heavily in state-of-the-art galvanizing and finishing facilities close to these hub assembly facilities. While some claim the Japanese investments in the U.S. steel industry are a positive outcome of trade restrictions, the real reason for these investments was to provide high-quality steel to the automotive transplants. In a number of cases, assembly transplants became so disgruntled with the low quality of the finished steel produced by traditional American steel makers that they asked their Japanese steel suppliers to relocate to America.[5]

All in all, Japanese investment in the United States demonstrates the transforming power of foreign investment. The industrial Midwest provides the prime example. This region, cast aside by many as a rust belt or a center of industrial decline, is today the nation's export belt and one of the world's most competitive manufacturing areas for autos and consumer electronics. Thanks to the inflow of international investment, the United States has witnessed an economic miracle of sorts.[6]

Europe, by contrast, provides an example of what the United States can expect from investment protectionism. For the past decade, Europeans have attempted to limit international investment, and in the process they have managed to forestall the industrial restructuring that the United States experienced in the 1980s. They are now paying the price, as their companies scramble to meet the tests of global competition. Protectionism has hurt the competitiveness of the European steel, auto, and computer industries.

Instead of emulating these mistakes and erecting barriers, U.S. policy makers—particularly those in Congress—should stop the drift toward conditional national treatment. CNT is a bad idea. It undermines the GATT, and it creates a break with the past. In the end, it will hurt us badly. The United States must try to maintain an attractive place for global capital, technology, and management. Only then will American managers and workers be able to compete in the 1990s and beyond.

4

Not All Investment Is the Same

Clyde V. Prestowitz, Jr.

The debate over investment policy is really an extension of the continuing trade debate, and of the "rocky coast" argument in particular. Also known as the unilateral free trade theory, this argument contends that if your trading partner is stupid enough to put rocks in his harbor such that he cannot import goods, you should not put rocks in your own. Trade, we are told, is invariably good. Even if your trading partner is unenlightened and still protects his workers, you should not be so backward as to do that yourself.

Composition Matters

The fundamental issue is not whether trade is good, but rather what type of trade or investment is good for the economy. The laissez-faire theory assumes that the structure of the economy and the composition of trade flows do not matter. In Washington and elsewhere, for example, some still believe that it does not matter for long-term productivity and economic welfare whether a company makes computer chips, wood chips, chocolate chips, or potato chips. But if it really does not matter what the economy produces, because all goods have essentially the same economic impact, then the discussion about the conditions of trade and investment is nonsense. Any discussion about trade barriers and unfair trade is a waste of time.

Consider the aircraft industry and the long-running dispute between the United States and Europe over Airbus. Central to that dispute is the assumption that it matters whether or not we make aircraft in the United States. If we did not hold that view, we would not be concerned with the European subsidies of Airbus. These subsidies allow the Europeans to sell aircraft to the American airlines below cost. According to the unilateral free trade argument, this arrangement should be treated as a gift to American carriers and presumably to American passengers. There are dislocation costs associated with this gift, however, which are imposed on the people at Boeing, McDonnell Douglas, and other companies who may thus be put out of work. Unilateral free traders argue, "Don't worry; up in Seattle they can become lumberjacks and make wood chips, and in St. Louis they can become brewers and make beer."

But if the structure of an economy significantly influences productivity and long-term economic welfare, then the composition of trade and investment flows does matter. Making wood chips does not generate the same benefit for the domestic economy as making airplanes. The conditions under which airplanes and products from other critical industries are made and traded, as a result, have to be examined more carefully.

Zero-Sum Trade and Investment

The issue therefore is not whether foreign investment is good or bad. Indeed, there is no inherent reason why a foreign investor cannot have the same positive impact on an economy as a domestic investor has. But investments are not all the same. There are different types of investment, just as there are different types of trade.

In the case of trade, it can be mutually beneficial and based on comparative advantage, as when we sell aircraft to the Costa Ricans and we import bananas from them. But there is also the zero-sum version of trade, in which the United States and Europe both try to sell aircraft to Saudi Arabia. One side will get the order and the jobs, while the other side will lose them. In this case, conditions of trade such as subsidies and access to the Saudi royal family matter, because they will influence who wins.

In the case of investments, too, there are positive and negative forms. Some investors want to be close to customers, sources of technology, or a better labor pool. Such investment can be very positive, as in the case of the Dutch company Philips, the largest producer of television sets in the United States. Philips is a "good corporate citizen," because it does most of its TV design and R&D activity in the United States, it creates products with high U.S. content, and it creates many jobs for American workers.

The steel industry provides another positive example of foreign direct investment. Over the past ten to fifteen years, foreign firms have invested significantly in the industry, transferring advanced technology and helping to revive the troubled U.S. steel industry. By all accounts, foreign investment has had a net positive impact. Interestingly, a somewhat restrictive trade policy prompted this investment. The investment did not just happen when the Japanese wanted to buy part of U.S. Steel. It happened because the United States moved to curtail the dumping of steel into the American market by negotiating a steel agreement that limited imports. The signal was clear: if foreign firms want to compete in U.S. markets, they must first invest.

It is also important to note the negative forms of investment. Those who are involved in shaping corporate strategy know that key questions must be examined before an investment decision is made: Should we buy our competitor and close him down? Should we buy our competitor's distributors and deprive him of the ability to distribute? Or should we dump our product in a foreign market, to drive local competitors to sell to us at a cut-rate price? Just as there are different strategies, there are different economic consequences for the domestic economy. In some cases, as when jobs are transferred abroad, the net impact of foreign direct investment will be negative.

Take the recent example of British Airways's buying into USAir and KLM's buying into Northwest. This should not be happening—the high-cost producers are taking over the low-cost producers. All the U.S. airlines are lower cost and more efficient. The average cost per seat mile for British Airways is 13.6 cents and for KLM 17.1 cents, as compared with USAir's 10.7 cents and Northwest's 9.3 cents.[1]

Subsidies and Investment Conditions Matter

As a high-cost producer, British Airways is able to invest in USAir only because of its protected base in Europe. At the Economic Strategy Institute, we have termed this phenomenon the Jurassic Park effect: the inefficient dinosaurs, who are protected and subsidized, are gaining control of the playground that the more efficient players, the U.S. airlines, would otherwise control.

The problem is that American carriers cannot buy into British Airways because they do not have free entry into either the British or the European markets. British law has a 25 percent ownership limitation and the Economic Community (EC), which must review any foreign investment in an EC airline, is unlikely to allow any foreign investment that threatens control of an airline.[2] This causes investment to occur on a nonreciprocal basis, under conditions that are more favorable to one side. When British Airways buys into USAir, it immediately extends its reach beyond the gateway city to 190 other American cities. With that reach, British Airways develops a superior international route system that gives it a competitive advantage over its American rivals: customers traveling to Europe can choose to bypass U.S. carriers in order to go straight through to London on British Airways. Jobs may then be transferred offshore as more flight attendants and pilots work for British Airways, while United, American, and Delta are forced to cut back.

The Real World Demands a Crowbar

The proper U.S. response is not to halt foreign investment, but to pay close attention to the conditions under which it takes place. The goal should be to maximize the potential positives and to minimize the negatives. Virtually every other country in the world already takes this approach, and it need not hurt. The Japanese, Korean, Taiwanese, Malayan, and Thai economies—despite their restrictions on investment—have performed tremendously well over the past twenty years. Indeed, Japan is the country least receptive to foreign investment, with the stock of foreign investment close to a rounding error in statistics. This is not an argument against foreign investment. Nor is it an argument for restrictions on foreign investment. Rather, it is an argument that a conditional policy on investment can be both practical and positive for the American economy.

The United States will inevitably face the question of whether we want to insist on broad reciprocity regarding investment-related issues. National treatment is also not always the best policy. Take telecommunications and the Uruguay Round. We did not push for national treatment, because countries like France have a telecommunications monopoly and we do not. National treatment under these conditions could, as a result, have negative consequences for the United States. The French could say, for example, "We will give you national treatment," which would mean that we could not invest in or sell to the French telecommunications industry, while national treatment in the United States translates into French firms' investing, selling, and licensing American technology. Clearly those circumstances would create very unequal competitive conditions between our telecommunications industry and theirs. The U.S. negotiating team was correct to back away from national treatment.

In an ideal world, there would be no restrictions on either investment or trade, and the United States would win in areas like airline service because we have the world's most efficient companies. But we do not live in that world, and asking for open skies and markets will not work, because nobody else wants them. Unilaterally opening U.S. markets without reciprocal access would be disadvantageous to the U.S. airline industry. Foreign airlines should be prevented from investing in or code-sharing with U.S. airlines until reciprocal rights combined with open skies can be implemented. Negotiations should ensure equal exchange of opportunity. In the case of Europe, no one country can deliver more than a fraction of the market. The negotiations therefore must be conducted with the European Community, to provide access to destinations throughout Europe and beyond in return for access to the United States.

A laissez-faire investment policy, in which we allow foreign airlines to buy up our airlines but we do not have reciprocal access, would also diminish our leverage in international negotiations. The real question is not the objective of these negotiations, but the leverage behind the U.S. position. Without something other than a laissez-faire investment policy, how will we get the leverage required to reduce trade barriers abroad? If Daimler-Benz and other European firms who want to operate in the United States are concerned about the directional change of U.S. policy, they can speak to the Deutsche Bank as well as to the European Union about reducing the restrictions on foreign investment in Germany and elsewhere in Europe.

5

Negotiate, Don't Legislate Reciprocity

Daniel M. Price

The broader competitiveness policy debate provides an important vehicle for the debate over investment and the treatment of domestic and foreign-owned firms operating in the United States.

Conditional National Treatment

There are more than twelve bills pending in Congress that seek to boost technological development and the economic welfare of American firms by making federal funds and facilities available to the private sector. These include the National Competitiveness Act, the Department of Energy Laboratory Technology Act, and the Environmental Technologies Act. To be eligible for any of the programs, a firm must first pass a two-part eligibility test. Part one consists of a general benefits test that requires both U.S.-owned and foreign-owned companies to demonstrate that their participation would be in the economic interest of the United States. Part two applies only to foreign-owned companies. It requires, in addition to the benefits test, that the company demonstrate that its home country government (1) has an open and nondiscriminatory investment environment; (2) grants U.S.-owned companies reciprocal access to comparable R&D programs; (3) provides adequate and effective intellectual property protection; and the list may go on.

No one takes issue with the view that U.S. tax dollars should be spent to benefit the American economy. At issue, instead, is whether the imposition of performance requirements and conditioning of national treatment are the proper policy tools to address problems of market access and discriminatory practices that U.S. investors may face abroad. The answer to the first is clearly "No"—performance

45

requirements impair U.S. competitiveness and are contrary to the global character of competitive enterprises. Today, we address the second question: In the inexorable search for leverage by Congress and U.S. negotiators, should federal R&D programs be used as a tool in the larger international trade and investment arena?

The Wrong Tool

The answer to that question is also "No." Conditional national treatment is not the proper tool for two reasons. First, it deprives the United States of the benefits of foreign direct investment: jobs, exports, technology, and new management techniques. Second, erecting barriers to foreign participation in technology programs may have the perverse effect of excluding those companies whose presence would otherwise give U.S.-owned firms access to useful foreign technology. Such barriers curtail the ability of U.S.-owned firms to form strategic alliances and to honor mutually beneficial cross-licensing agreements—a key part of doing business in today's global arena. Joint ventures and strategic alliances, if properly structured, are generally viewed as enhancing competitiveness and investment flows. But the CNT provisions discourage such partnerships by artificially increasing the risk associated with entering a relationship with a foreign-owned firm. Even if the firm is a model corporate citizen—investing in domestic R&D and production—its home government may still not pass the latest U.S. CNT test, and therefore the firm may jeopardize its American partner's chances for an R&D grant or antitrust exemption or some other advantage.

The Manton Amendment and the Spread of CNT

Performance requirements and the CNT provisions challenge the principle of national treatment that the United States has traditionally upheld and most recently advanced in the NAFTA agreement. Performance requirements may also impede the competitiveness of U.S.-based enterprises. Take, for example, the Manton amendment to the National Competitiveness Act.[1] To be eligible for the Department of Commerce technology programs, the Manton amendment would require both U.S.-owned and foreign-owned firms to commit to using only American parts and supplies in the manufacture of any product made from the technology developed under the grant. Products incorporating that technology must also be manufactured in the United States—regardless of the existence of a foreign affiliate and regardless of how a particular piece of technology fits into a company's general manufacturing scheme. It must be manufactured in the United States.

Such performance requirements defeat the purpose of technology policy and fail to reflect the globalization of business. If the purpose is to promote the competitiveness of enterprises in the United States and the innovation of U.S.-based technology, it does not make sense to draw fences around technological developments. A firm cannot promise today that no matter what direction the innovation process takes, it will only use a technology in its American facilities. Likewise, a company cannot promise to procure all its supplies from American companies. Presented with such a choice, innovative American-owned and foreign-owned firms may be unwilling to risk their flexibility or mortgage their technological futures to participate in a federal program.

The Manton amendment is another step in a series of new laws and congressional proposals aimed at instituting a reciprocity standard for foreign investors. It would institute a harsher conditional national treatment test than already exists under current law. As in the existing Advanced Technology Program (ATP) language, the Manton amendment would require the government of a foreign-owned firm to pass a reciprocity test before the firm would be eligible for the ATP program. But the test would be extended to include a mirror-image reciprocity requirement that the home government of the foreign firm provide access to technology programs equivalent to the expanded ATP. Manton would also add a fourth criterion to the existing reciprocity checklist, by requiring that the home government maintain a "standards development and conformity assessment process that is open and transparent, and that results in standards that are fair and reasonable and that do not discriminate against United States products and production processes." Fair treatment of U.S. companies and products is a fundamental policy objective, but we should not deprive ourselves of the benefits of foreign participation by attempting to legislate outcomes that must be negotiated.

Perhaps most important, the Manton amendment should be viewed by U.S. policy makers as a fundamental challenge to look beyond specific technology programs and industry examples to examine the hazards presented by the larger CNT trend. If unchecked, the CNT approach will inevitably spread. It has no natural boundaries. To date, those pushing the CNT approach have focused their efforts on instituting the three-part CNT test for most of the federal programs that make up the technology policy agenda. But as the Manton amendment to the National Competitiveness Act indicates, there is pressure for the CNT wish list to grow. In addition to the three original reciprocity conditions, in the future foreign-owned firms may be penalized for the practices of their home governments in the areas of standards (Manton), antitrust regulations, and food and drug regulations, as well as any new area of trade friction that may arise. Whenever the government can hand out a benefit or lessen a burden, it can also extract something from the recipient. Technology policy and government-sponsored programs thus provide an unfortunate platform onto which the CNT list of requirements can readily spread in a misguided effort to advance the latest trade policy flavor *du jour*.

Credible Alternatives Exist

Two steps will help to address the root problems underlying the Manton amendment and the appeal of the conditional national treatment approach in Congress. First, this debate reflects the need for the private sector to explain the competitive demands of today's global environment to policy makers in both the legislative and the executive branches. Not enough time or attention has been devoted to this education task: Why is it that a U.S. company needs technology from a foreign company? Why does a foreign-owned firm want technology through a cross-licensing arrangement with a U.S. company? More must be done to answer these questions for U.S. policy makers and to educate them on the critical, continuing need for deep relationships with companies around the world. The reality is that competitive companies manufacture, source, and develop technology on a global basis. Our laws and policies must reflect, not impede, what our companies have to do to compete.

Second, the administration must become more involved. Its opposition to the Manton amendment was a good start, but a strong, clear policy statement on foreign investment is needed to address the other CNT proposals pending in Congress. Investment dispute mechanisms also must be developed with our trading partners. The problem of conditional national treatment cannot be solved simply by having all parties promising to abstain. Every investment agreement negotiation in which I have ever participated, including NAFTA and bilateral investment treaties, or that I have observed, has begun with the exchange of national treatment promises and concluded with a list of exceptions. The United States must move beyond this approach, examine the list of exceptions, and choose the sectors where it can reach an agreement.

Rather than trying to resolve differences by legislative fiat, we should employ negotiation and a series of incremental steps. The choice is not between unilateral free trade or laissez faire and intervention. The issue is *how* the United States should address discriminatory practices abroad. How can we advance our economic interests in further opening markets abroad without curtailing our interests in promoting foreign direct investment at home?

If eligibility requirements in technology programs are a problem, for example, then let the administrators of those programs in the given countries work out a common framework to ensure that those programs are open to all. In the case of Europe, once there is a transatlantic mechanism and a history of solving problems, then it may be productive to enlarge the framework, as in the Organization for Economic Cooperation and Development (OECD) multilateral investment agreement mechanism. Until then, the U.S. government should, as I believe the State Department and U.S.T.R. are already doing, work in the OECD to enlarge the investment discussions and to open a dialogue with non-OECD countries or with subsets of OECD countries. We should learn from our experience in the Uruguay Round and in the European Energy Charter: it makes sense to sit down and talk to each other about problems before they blow up in larger settings.

The time is ripe. Out of their own self-interest, developing countries are moving away from excessive regulation and investment restrictions. The Clinton administration must resist the pressure to move in the opposite direction. Indeed, it is ironic that just as we have gotten Mexico to agree under NAFTA to limit performance requirements (to forgo the right to impose domestic content requirements as a condition for a firm to serve the world market from Mexico, for example), the United States has begun to backtrack. The wide-ranging telecommunications bill (H.R. 3626) that would deregulate the industry, for example, tells the Baby Bells that they can get involved in manufacturing, provided all the manufacturing is done here and all components are sourced here.

Rather than experimenting with such restrictions—whether under the Manton amendment or the deregulation of the telecommunications industry—the United States should focus on setting aside false conflicts. Instead of asking who benefits the United States more, the government should adopt policies that maximize the contributions to the domestic economy of both foreign-owned and U.S.-owned businesses. We must avoid aiming a gun at our heads and saying, "Open your markets or I'll shoot!"

6

Use a Different Lever

Ellen L. Frost

The extension of the global economy and the accompanying change in corporate behavior have brought investment and conditional national treatment to the front of the policy debate. It is essential for the private sector to play an active role in this debate, to redefine the terms, and to educate us all about the benefits at stake.

We must also maintain a dynamic perspective. Other countries have behaved differently from the United States in investment. But we are witnessing a sea change, especially in developing countries. In the Asia-Pacific region and in Latin America, one country after another is moving to deregulate, privatize, and reduce restrictions on investment. This is a business-driven movement, a historical trend pushed by market forces that may be irreversible. The first Vietnamese delegation has now appeared in the office of the U.S. Trade Representative (USTR), for example, hungry to learn more about U.S. views on trade and investment policies.

We Need Foreign Investment

Speaking for the administration, I can make a clear, strong policy statement: We support an open investment climate. Trade and investment increasingly are inseparable. We do not associate foreign investment with the export of U.S. jobs. Instead, with so many of our exports going to investment in U.S. subsidiaries abroad, we view investment flows as closely tied to exports.

The Clinton administration also welcomes foreign investment in the United States, not only because it is good for us but also because we need foreign capital. In the 1980s, the U.S. investment-savings gap of roughly a trillion dollars was largely filled by foreign investors. Today, the need continues as we grow faster than our allies, and the trade deficit increases as a result. Foreign investors

51

must also be viewed in the dynamic context of the changing U.S. labor market. The central goal of the Clinton administration is to increase the number of high-wage jobs. Both inward and outward investment flows encourage the economic adjustment needed to meet the new competition and accomplish this objective. Two related signs of this adjustment are the trend toward cross-licensing and the geographic diversification of production. Awareness of these changes is widespread and growing within the administration.

Technology Policy Is the Wrong Lever

The reasons detailed above for favoring an open investment climate have led the administration to oppose the Manton amendment to the National Competitiveness Act as a step that would seriously undermine the objectives of the act.

When there is taxpayer money at stake, as in the technology programs, it is reasonable to look for benefits to the nation. But in defining how "national benefits" should be interpreted, we have told Congress that we support a flexible interpretation.[1] Reliance on mechanistic criteria can backfire and prevent us from ensuring that taxpayer investment in R&D provides the greatest possible benefit to the American economy. It may, for example, inhibit participation of those very firms that will create jobs. Small and medium-sized firms may be particularly disadvantaged in their efforts to participate by the excessive regulatory burdens imposed.

For these reasons we do not support mandating reciprocity through a legislative option, whether or not it is sector-specific—just the opposite. We have an existing set of trade tools to handle market-access barriers that concern the United States. We do not need specific reciprocity language in R&D contracts. Everyone at USTR wants to break down investment and other trade barriers, but it does not make sense to deny a good R&D project because of a narrow reciprocity requirement. Indeed, the effect could be negative. Why cut off your nose to spite your face? We have sufficient authority in section 301 of the trade law to exert leverage on a foreign country that does not maintain an open investment climate. After all, leverage is the middle name of every USTR negotiator. Another investment-specific tool is section 307 of the 1984 Trade Act.

The old-new issue of investment, a priority for the administration, is on the post–Uruguay Round agenda that will also deal with the new issues of the environment and labor standards. The Uruguay Round talks on trade-related investment measures (TRIMs) were a start, but they did not go as far as we would like.[2] Investment is an emotional and volatile issue. In the near term, it will not be easy to reach agreement on investment with the 117 countries that signed the Uruguay Round last April and with more than 20 trying to join the GATT or its successor, the World Trade Organization.

As a result, we will be forced to operate on three tracks. In addition to the multilateral talks, we would like to expand both regional and bilateral investment activities when appropriate. The Asia Pacific Economic Cooperation (APEC)[3] discussion on non-binding investment may prove beneficial, but it is a preliminary and long-term effort, fraught with diplomatic sensitivities. Regarding the Organization for Economic Cooperation and Development (OECD) wider investment instrument, USTR would like to set high standards and thereby limit the danger of reaching an agreement for the sake of reaching an agreement. We did achieve high investment standards in the NAFTA, and we would like to see something like that extended. Bilateral investment treaties with individual countries are another avenue we will continue to pursue.

A Positive Investment Agenda

Finally, the United States must put a positive agenda on the table. Often we sit around talking about the use of Super 301[4] of the trade law or of Special 301's provisions on intellectual property. Instead of interacting only on a punitive level, the United States must work more with developing countries in a collegial spirit, helping them to write laws and responding to their legitimate concerns in a constructive manner.

Sometimes we also exaggerate our own leverage. Our share of world trade is getting smaller as other countries are participating more in international markets, and we are becoming increasingly dependent on trade as a share of total GNP. Although we are still the biggest market in the world—so we do have *some* leverage—we need a positive agenda for the future. On the domestic front, U.S. policy must also respond to the needs of workers displaced by any form of competitive adjustment—even those not related to trade. As we stand back and look at investment in a broader context, we must not leave out the human element.

7

How Do We Move Forward?
A Discussion

Conditional National Treatment

HARRY FREEMAN, Freeman & Company: Mr. Florida, the European Commission issued three directives (in banking, securities, and insurance) between 1989 and 1991 that required reciprocity. If the United States does not let German or French financial services into these areas, then American firms will be restricted in their offer of financial services in Europe. After the European Union also refused U.S. proposals in the Uruguay Round for an open regime, Congress responded by introducing the Fair Trade in Financial Services bill, which calls for reciprocity in financial services. Why do you oppose this bill? Why should the Europeans be nervous about reciprocity mandates in the United States when it is at the base of their proposed financial system?

RICHARD FLORIDA, Center for Economic Development, Carnegie Mellon University: The objective of U.S. trade and investment policy, we all agree, is to reap the fruits of globalization whether it be in manufacturing or in financial services, where there are barriers to competition. The question is whether we want to pursue this objective by taking a step backward to reciprocity and conditioning national treatment or whether we want to move in a positive direction.

In financial services, the United States has to develop a positive agenda. Instead of the tit-for-tat approach, the emphasis should be on developing a broader multilateral mechanism. In some sectors, the United States has already tested the waters but frequently makes a tactical retreat. We would gain both bilaterally and multilaterally from embracing a positive agenda consistently.

CLYDE V. PRESTOWITZ, JR., Economic Strategy Institute: But what is the positive agenda? Would you go to Europeans, who have staked out their position, to try to persuade them to open their market without threatening them with any reciprocal action? In practice, this action allows them to do whatever they want to do in our market, while we sit on the sidelines in their market. What would you use to induce them to open up?

MR. FLORIDA: There are two ways to gain leverage: either we try strong-arm tactics, as Mr. Prestowitz suggests, or we try to build coalitions with other countries, such as Britain. Building a coalition, in my opinion, would be the best strategy for the United States. The United States should also support private investment initiatives because strategic alliances, joint ventures, and the like circumvent barriers more effectively than governments' efforts to make economic gains at the expense of others. Throughout history, investors have overcome national barriers by investing in other markets. Reciprocal treatment is not needed—and over the long run it will not work.

ELLEN L. FROST, counselor to the U.S. trade representative: If we want to deny access to our market to gain leverage, we have many other tools to use. We do not have to use federally funded R&D programs to accomplish this objective.

MODERATOR: So you would still take the approach of mandating reciprocity through a legislative option outside of the federally funded R&D programs?

MS. FROST: No. If we are concerned about a market access barrier in another country, we have an existing set of trade tools to handle it. We do not have to place specific reciprocity language in R&D contracts or anything of the sort.

DANIEL M. PRICE, Powell, Goldstein, Frazer, and Murphy: Besides, the legislative approach or the conditional national treatment (CNT) legal test is inadequate to address the problems on the table. In Europe, for example, the United States needs to address the assumption present in any transatlantic discussion, namely, that unless common ground is negotiated, the playing field may not be level.

Take eligibility requirements. The assumption is that if we do not together agree on common eligibility criteria, the criteria will differ with potentially damaging consequences. The CNT legal test does nothing to resolve the problem of defining common criteria. The structure proposes instead that before Congress lets an investor into the United States, that investor must satisfy American reciprocity definitions plus the trade policy flavor *du jour*. A more productive discussion—one focused not on securing the primary benefits of an R&D program for a given country but rather on defining a mutually acceptable minimum set of rules—could take place at the agency level.

STEVEN CANNER, at U.S. Treasury Department, formerly with the Office of Investment: First, we clearly need foreign investment. We are saving only 2 percent of our gross domestic product a year, which requires us to use other people's money to maintain a high-growth economy. If we could save more, as we did in the 1950s, then we would have another option. Until that happens, we need foreign investment.

Second, it is important to note the differences between the "use another crowbar" approach advocated by Ellen Frost and the transaction-oriented approach pushed by Clyde Prestowitz. The implications differ substantially for the shape of policy and how it is carried out. For example, "the other crowbar" approach would aim at opening markets, leaving individual transactions to be decided by investors. The transaction-oriented approach implies government approval of which investments are "good" and which are not. Clearly, we must reject the transaction-oriented approach.

Asia and China

LAURA MOORHEAD, executive director, Organization for International Investment: When do you believe the Europeans and others will have a clear understanding of the consequences and dynamics of globalization?

MR. PRESTOWITZ: The Europeans are not the problem. In June, I heard a speech that Mr. Mahattir gave in Kuala Lumpur, Malaysia, on the evils of Fortress Europe, comparing the rules for investing in Malaysia with those for Europe. He found it much easier to invest in Europe, even though there are some restrictions. But a person can invest or make an acquisition in Europe if he wants to. In fact, American corporations have invested roughly $450 billion in Europe. For the most part, the Europeans are moving in our direction.

The real challenge is northern Asia: there is virtually no foreign investment in Japan and very little in Korea. Every Asian country, even free countries like Singapore, regulates investment much more than we do. All the Asian countries maintain some type of regulatory investment environment with substantial government involvement. To participate in the local economy, all require, by one means or another, investment in the domestic market. Mandatory joint ventures and technology transfer are but two of the tools.

China is probably the best example. To get into the Chinese market, American CEOs are required to enter joint ventures and to transfer technology. But according to the laissez-faire theory, rather than enforce such restrictions, the Chinese should try to create the most attractive market possible. Yet, also contrary to the laissez-faire view, investors have not been frightened off; instead, they are flocking to China to line up their next joint venture partner.

I frankly do not see China or any of these countries changing their policies. Investing in Japan, Korea, and the others will, as a result, remain very difficult. Study after study demonstrates, for example, that trade follows investment as overseas subsidiaries import parts from the home country. To the extent that the rules of investment in China, Japan, or elsewhere require our companies to export from those foreign markets as a condition of investment, we will drive ourselves to a structural trade deficit. To solve the deficit, we will tell ourselves that we have to devalue the currency, which will then give us less purchasing power and influence in the world.

MR. PRICE: The Chinese example is indeed a good one because it demonstrates how *inadequate* reciprocity or the CNT crowbar approach is in a bilateral context. I suspect that American negotiators would like nothing better than to require China to sign a bilateral investment treaty in which local equity, export, and performance requirements were prohibited. But in the case of China, mandating reciprocity through legislation contributes little to the goal. We cannot say to the Chinese, "Listen, if you don't agree to prohibit performance requirements, we will impose similar requirements on your investments here," because they do not invest here to a significant extent. Other tools will have to be used to gain effective leverage over the Chinese.

MS. FROST: The United States recently took action against China on intellectual property, for example, under the Special 301 trade law.

In July, U.S. Trade Representative Mickey Kantor named China as a priority foreign country, which means that China could be subjected to trade sanctions equivalent to the estimated lost sales (roughly $480 million a year) of U.S. companies due to lax enforcement of laws protecting intellectual property. After the six- to nine-month investigation of China, if there is no resolution of American concerns, the United States could initiate sanctions.[1]

Trade sanctions aimed at their exports, in my opinion, are likely to be a more cost-effective approach to resolving U.S. concerns than trying to restrict foreign investment in the United States. Although I would want to review the sanctions first, the United States could presumably threaten a trade sanction rather than resort to a tit-for-tat sector-specific reciprocity measure. Instead of mechanistic or rigid criteria, the goal is to be as free as possible to choose the most effective negotiating tool available.

MR. FLORIDA: But why do we want to emulate bad policy? If a nation wants to restrict foreign investment, which is the source of new technology, best-practice management, and innovation stimulants to the local economy, then let it. Why would we want to emulate counterproductive policies?

CHARLES WESSNER, consultant on technology and communications policy: Why should we assume that "poor" countries like Japan and France with counterproductive policies don't understand? Is that not an almost academic perspective? Their growth rates do not suggest misguided policies. On the R&D issue, the Europeans have longstanding programs restricted primarily to European countries. They let IBM into Jessi only when they could not make the chips that they needed for their own programs. Equality of access and equal participation will not come about unless there are criteria for these programs.

MR. PRICE: Common criteria—not no criteria—should be a goal. But one can shape these criteria for participation by both U.S.-owned and foreign-owned companies such that it is nationality neutral and the national treatment principle is preserved. The criteria would allow tax dollars to promote benefits for the domestic economy without imposing counterproductive CNT measures. In order to ensure U.S. access to foreign programs, rather than adopt the heavy-handed approach illustrated most recently by the Manton amendment, the administrators should get together and work out common eligibility criteria.

TODD MALAN, European-American Chamber of Commerce: It may help to look at the actual numbers or data and thereby correct some impressions that Mr. Wessner had about access to European R&D programs. In a recent audit of American companies participating in European programs, the Chamber of Commerce found seventy-six American companies involved in the full range of European Union programs. The Fourth Framework directive pending before the European Commission also has no restriction in it regarding foreign participation. On the U.S. side, by contrast, only two foreign-owned companies participate in the U.S. Advanced Technology program in the Department of Commerce.

LARRY FULLERTON, Powell, Goldstein, Frazer, and Murphy: In the interest of full disclosure, I represent British Airways. I would like to correct five misguided statements on the regulation of foreign investment and the British Airways investment in USAir.

First, Clyde Prestowitz implied that British Airways is subsidized. It is not: it is a private company that is publicly traded, neither owned by the government nor subsidized. Second, it is not the case that the British government will not permit a reciprocal investment transaction. Today, over 40 percent of British Airways is foreign owned with over 20 percent owned by individual U.S. investors. On numerous occasions, John McGregor, U.K. secretary of state transport, has said specifically that he would approve a reverse transaction. Third, European investment rules are not more restrictive than American rules on foreign investment in air carriers. It is quite the opposite: European rules are more liberal. Under the European rules, foreigners can own up to 49 percent of European air carriers and exercise all of that as voting rights. U.S. rules impose a 25 percent voting limit and a 49 percent equity limit. In both cases, there is a de facto control test.

Fourth, on the jobs question, the British Airways investment in USAir has not had the negative impact of exporting American jobs that Mr. Prestowitz suggested. If British Airways designs a successful marketing device for routes from the United States to Europe, then we will see a shift of passengers from American to British carriers. But the employment impact of this shift is not clear cut. One may tend to assume that more passengers on U.S. carriers translates into more American jobs, but this is not always the case. Both British and U.S. carriers employ people on both sides of the Atlantic. British Airways has 2,000 employees in the United States, and U.S. carriers presumably have a similar number of employees in Europe to service and load passengers onto the planes. As market share shifts, the distribution of employees across the two carriers shifts, but that shift does not necessarily cause U.S. jobs to be lost. A casual reading of the press would also suggest that the British Airways investment in USAir has played a positive role in saving roughly 47,000 jobs at USAir.

Fifth, I take issue with Mr. Prestowitz's assumption that the U.S. policy is for open skies in the United States. While one aim of U.S. policy is clearly to improve the market share of U.S. carriers by expanding their right to fly to foreign destinations, that aim is not the same as an open-skies policy that includes the skies over the United States. From my review of the public statements of U.S. air carriers, I can assure you that their goal is not open skies.

MR. PRESTOWITZ: Much of what Mr. Fullerton said is correct: British Airways is not currently subsidized; it is a private company; and it does have foreign investment. Those investors are not airlines, though, but individuals like you and me. The British Airways sheet, however, was cleaned up nicely as the company was transformed from a government entity into a private entity. It is also protected, along with the entire European air market, behind a screen that allows British Airways to dominate Heathrow Airport in London. It is worth your eye teeth to get a slot at Heathrow. Perhaps, as suggested, the British government would accept reciprocal investment. But under the European Union rules, the European Commission needs to approve the transaction. France has already made it clear that any strategic investment by a foreign airline in a European airline would be challenged. The British are therefore safe hiding behind the French.

On the jobs issue, because British Airways hires Americans, some jobs were saved that might otherwise have been lost at USAir. But if jobs at USAir were saved because Delta, American, and United lost them, then this substitution effect needs to be taken into account. Then, I believe, the U.S. economy is not likely to register a net increase in employment from foreign investment. What is clear is that the maintenance and headquarters jobs will go where the airline is based. Therefore, it seems reasonable to assume a transfer of jobs overseas.

Congress versus the Administration

HOWARD ROSEN, Competitiveness Policy Council: First, because our net savings rate fell last year and our personal savings are at a historical low, the only way we can increase our job base in this country is either to reduce our consumption or to borrow foreign capital to invest in jobs.

Second, performance requirements are not a very good approach for tying down investment. But if other countries set them, our best hope of getting rid of these requirements is to negotiate from a position of strength. Does the Manton amendment build U.S. strength, and should the administration or Congress take the lead through something like the Manton amendment in negotiating with our trading partners?

MR. PRESTOWITZ: I am not arguing for the Manton amendment. But clearly a unilateral laissez-faire policy will make it very difficult to negotiate a more even-handed international investment regime. We need some tools to induce investment.

In an ideal world, administrative procedures such as reciprocal application of regulatory procedures are preferable to legislation. But the legislation option has been chosen because legislators have lost hope that the administration will use those tools. There are always a thousand reasons why we hesitate to take some kind of administrative measure. Whether these issues come up in a Democratic or in a Republican administration, we always need somebody's help in the Persian Gulf or with the North Koreans or with a vote at the United Nations. Typically, the argument in these debates is, for example, why endanger the whole Korean Peninsula for a few dollars. Economic considerations accordingly are subordinated to foreign policy concerns. Out of frustration, legislators have turned to legislation to mandate that something be done. Although, of course, care must be taken, I believe the legislative approach is probably preferable and practical.

MR. PRICE: The performance requirements in the U.S. R&D programs and the Manton amendment simply have no place. They do not build strength but just the opposite. We need to remember the purpose of much of the CNT legislation, namely, to enhance the competitiveness of enterprises operating in the United States—American or foreign-owned. But to be successful in this endeavor, we ought to be observant. If our most technologically sophisticated companies respond to the eligibility requirements by not participating, what good can the program accomplish? Foreign participation is necessary if the United States is to develop a cutting-edge technology base. The CNT legislation tries to accomplish too many goals at once and, as a result, risks accomplishing nothing.

MODERATOR: As the panel has suggested, there is clearly more than one way to gain leverage in international negotiations. The challenge is to gain and exercise that leverage in a cost-effective manner to advance American economic interests at home and abroad. In the area of investment, the specific challenge is both to encourage foreign direct investment in the United States *and* to curtail discriminatory practices against U.S. investors abroad. As the panel has also demonstrated, the conditional national treatment approach pits these two worthwhile objectives against each other. A foreign-owned firm may pass, for example, the so-called good corporate citizen test by doing substantial R&D and production in the United States and yet still be treated as a second-class citizen because the intellectual property or standards practices of its home government fail to pass the good country definition of U.S. legislators.

The research and business communities have an important role to play in educating and working with policy makers in Congress and the administration to circumvent this CNT dilemma of having to choose one worthwhile objective at the expense of another. By opening the debate and providing some perspective on the trade-offs and the hazards of the CNT approach, this discussion has started the process. But there is much more to be done.

8

Foreign Direct Investment and the Economy

Richard Florida

American policy toward international investment is undergoing a dramatic shift. Long the world's most ardent advocate of unrestricted investment, the United States has traditionally opposed attempts by other nations to place conditions on investment, arguing that politics should not intrude on business decisions and undermine competition. There is, however, a growing movement in Congress to impose new restrictions and conditions on international investment, and technology policy is the preferred vehicle for this sort of investment protectionism.

Attempts by Congress to restrict international investment are out of touch with the demands of an increasingly global economy. Rapidly rising global investment by companies around the world has forever changed the nature of economic life. Investment is now more important than trade as a component of international business. Transnational corporations currently operate some 170,000 affiliates across the globe; this worldwide network of foreign affiliates generated more than \$5.5 trillion in world sales in 1990, a figure that exceeded world exports of \$4 trillion of goods and nonfactor services.[1]

The evidence is clear: international investment stands ever more clearly as a key determinant of domestic productivity and of economic success in the global economy. The inflows bring jobs as well as new technologies and management practices to the host country. The outflows enable companies to open markets abroad, generating exports in the form of intrafirm trade. The issue at stake in the debate over international investment should be the ability of an economy to attract it.

This chapter examines the role of foreign investment in the U.S. economy and recent trends in U.S. policy toward this investment. It begins with a review of U.S. policy, highlighting the key pieces of legislation that attempt to impose conditions (performance requirements or other types of restrictions on foreign investment) and outlining the major assumptions upon which such investment protectionism is premised. The second section examines the increasingly important role played by international investment in the American economy and the larger global economy. A new theory is offered that identifies a clear link between international investment and productivity and employment growth. Particular attention is paid to the economic contribution of foreign investment in the areas of the technology base, job generation, and the economic revitalization of the Midwestern manufacturing belt. The chapter concludes with an outline for a multilateral investment agenda or GATT-like agreement on investment.

A Dangerous Drift in Policy

When it comes to having a liberal investment regime, the United States has led the world by example. For most of the modern, post–World War II era, the United States has generally refrained from putting conditions on international investment and has maintained instead a strong commitment to openness and neutrality.[2] This open-door policy was politically sustainable largely because the country and its leaders perceived that competition from foreign producers did not constitute a major threat to domestic industry.

American policy toward international investment has generally been based on adherence to the principle of equal treatment for all investors, which ensures that all firms operating in the United States are treated equally regardless of nationality of ownership. This principle means that foreign investors are treated the same as domestic investors under American laws. Equal treatment strengthens the U.S. economy by ensuring a stable international investment system, attracting foreign capital (and with it, jobs and technology) and, in theory, helping to protect U.S. investments in other countries. The practice of conferring most-favored nation treatment has also meant that a foreign-owned company receives treatment no less favorable than that accorded any other foreign-owned companies.

U.S. negotiators have generally insisted on adhering to these principles in NAFTA and in the continuing campaign to convince developing nations to enter into bilateral investment treaties with the United States. The United States has similarly challenged the use of trade-related investment measures by other nations, because such measures impose export requirements, local content demands, and technology conditions on firms.[3] The United States has even insisted on the adoption of a TRIMs code under the GATT, forbidding such practices.

Congress's commitment to equal treatment has waned in recent years. Beginning in the late 1980s, Congress started to consider and to pass legislation that imposes new requirements and conditions on international investors and foreign-owned firms in general, particularly foreign-affiliated companies that might wish to participate in federally funded technology programs. There are two principal components of this recent shift to a more restrictive policy regime toward international investment:

- *Conditional national treatment* links the treatment of foreign investors to the practices of their home country governments. Conditional national treatment is frequently defended as a tactical mechanism to open foreign markets.
- *Performance requirements* are the standards on domestic content, employment, or other performance goals. These are often nationality-neutral, applying to both domestically and foreign-owned firms.

Two additional components of the legislative shift toward a more protectionist posture on international investment are:

- *disclosure requirements* on operations and intended acquisitions of international affiliates
- *screening*, which is designed to evaluate the impact of international affiliates and potentially to block acquisitions on the grounds of national economic security[4]

Virtually all advanced economies place restrictions on international investment. In the United States, these laws affect the ownership of or rights to such things as agricultural property, banks, mineral leases and extraction, geothermal production, construction of deep-water ports, and production of nuclear energy.[5] The rationale for these restrictions is the protection of national security. During the early 1970s, however, Congress saw the need for greater control over international investment. This attention was aroused in large measure by the surge in portfolio investment from abroad, particularly from the OPEC nations. In response to this concern, the Ford administration signed an executive order in 1975 creating the Committee on Foreign Investment in the United States (CFIUS), an interagency group that tracks international investment and makes recommendations to the president.[6]

By the late 1980s, in the wake of a series of high-profile foreign acquisitions, congressional pressure mounted for additional restrictions to protect against foreign acquisitions of U.S. companies that owned or manufactured critical defense technologies. As part of the Omnibus Trade Bill of 1988, Congress passed the Exon-Florio amendments. The Exon-Florio provisions granted the president the authority to take whatever actions he deems appropriate to prevent foreign acquisitions of defense-related companies that would threaten or impair national security. President Reagan delegated this authority to CFIUS.[7] In 1988, the House appended the Omnibus Trade Bill with a provision known as the Bryant amendment. This measure would have required significant disclosure of information on the part of foreign investors if they intended to obtain more than 5 percent ownership of an American firm; the amendment would have required even more disclosure in the event that foreign ownership reached 20 percent. The provision did not survive conference, but it did pass the House as a free-standing bill.

In 1990, to mollify the concern that lay behind the Bryant amendment, the Bush administration proposed and signed a bill to improve the analysis and distribution of information on foreign investment that the federal government was already collecting. In effect, the law authorized the Census Bureau and the Bureau of Economic Analysis to make information available that, for reasons of confidentiality, they had previously kept to themselves. While Exon-Florio ultimately became a permanent federal law, as opposed to one requiring reauthorization, an attempt to extend Exon-Florio to cover national *economic* security—the acquisition of civilian high-technology companies—was unsuccessful. At last count, CFIUS had received more than 800 notifications of intent to invest in defense-related companies, and at least 15 cases had gone through the investigation. This resulted in only one proposal being blocked, however.[8]

In the early 1990s, congressional support for increased restrictions on foreign investment surged anew, turning to the more contentious and potentially more damaging issues of performance requirements and conditional national treatment (see table A–1). A number of recent pieces of federal technology policy legislation call for stringent performance requirements of both domestic and foreign-owned companies. This means that potential participants in federal programs must give evidence that they operate manufacturing facilities, conduct research and development, *or* maintain significant employment in the United States. Many of these bills seek to condition the participation of foreign-owned firms on the practices of their home governments, requiring that these nations provide comparable or equivalent opportunities for U.S.-owned companies to participate in programs abroad, and that they afford comparable investment opportunities and similar intellectual property protection to U.S. firms abroad.[9] Conditional national treatment is frequently defended as a tactical measure to open foreign markets to U.S. goods and services. The Congressional Office of Technology Assessment, for example, recently suggested that "selective reciprocity" could be used to provide leverage for the U.S. government in the task of promoting trade and investment by U.S. firms.[10]

The American Technology Preeminence Act of 1991 is a case in point. This legislation requires that participating foreign-owned companies conduct substantial R&D and manufacturing in the United States, and that they have a home government that allows U.S.-owned companies to participate in government-sponsored programs, affords local opportunities to U.S. companies, and gives U.S. firms suitable intellectual property protection. The language from this bill has found its way into further legislation for the development of critical technologies, manufacturing technologies, aerospace technologies, environmental technologies, space-exploration technologies, and defense technologies—just about the full gamut of technologies. In 1993, the House passed two similar amendments—the Manton and the Collins amendments to the National Competitiveness Act of 1993—which would create much tougher criteria for program participation by foreign-owned companies by requiring that their home governments provide U.S. firms with access to information and resources *equivalent* to those authorized under that act.

This protectionist drift in investment policy threatens not only a key source of domestic economic improvement but also the central principle of national treatment that is at the base of the modern global economy. It has not yet provoked retaliation from abroad. But if the drift persists, conflict will also increase with our trading partners, and foreign retaliation against U.S. multinationals abroad might ensue. The European Community has already threatened to invoke its version of conditional national treatment—the so-called Metten resolution, which bears striking similarity to the Manton amendment to the National Competitiveness Act—if U.S. policy moves further down the path to investment protectionism.[11] Such a policy showdown would be costly to all those involved and would potentially undermine the international flow of investment that has become the key feature of the new global economy. The Clinton administration, to its credit, has shown a willingness to reject the more restrictive proposals from the Congress on conditional national treatment. But the risks to the domestic and the global economy posed by the trend demand more. The United States must articulate a coherent policy toward international investment and economic globalization.

Shaky Concepts, Faulty Assumptions

The recent drift in Congress toward investment protectionism is based on a series of shaky concepts and faulty assumptions that provide an inappropriate rationale for policy. This view starts from the premise that international investment *injures* the U.S. economy in a number of ways: by eliminating high-wage jobs, by transferring U.S. technology to foreign competition, and by contributing to the trade deficit. As a consequence, government intervention is required to protect jobs, halt the flow of U.S. technology abroad, and maintain national economic security by ensuring that critical economic and technological assets are not controlled by foreign interests. This approach ignores the considerable contributions that international investment has made to the home economy, and it fails to recognize the fundamental trend toward the globalization of economic activity—a trend that federal legislation will be unable to curtail.

The debate over international investment, in particular, over the issue of performance requirements, has revolved around the faulty concept of corporate nationality. In an article published in the *Harvard Business Review* and later expanded in his book *The Work of Nations*, Robert Reich argued that corporate ownership is less important than the scope and nature of domestic activities those corporations undertake.[12] Posing the provocative question, "Who Is Us?" Reich suggested that international firms that invest in plant, equipment, and jobs in the United States may contribute more to domestic economic welfare than U.S.-owned companies that invest abroad. The chairperson of the Council of Economic Advisers, Laura Tyson, countered that corporate nationality continues to matter, insisting that foreign-owned companies "are not us."[13]

Although quite innocuous on the surface, this debate has done a great deal to undermine America's traditionally open investment regime. At the same time that Reich defends the concept of equal treatment, his argument has helped to fuel the fire for performance requirements by suggesting that a firm's contribution to the domestic economy can be measured by the level of investment, technology development, or employment it provides. The implication of this perspective is that the federal government should offer incentives for companies that place a considerable share of their assets and activities in the United States, while creating explicit disincentives or outright penalties for those that do not. Indeed, a highly controversial story in the *New York Times* reported that members of the Clinton administration had devised a crude performance-rating system for U.S. and international corporations based on the level of their activities in the United States.[14]

The implication of Tyson's argument goes further, suggesting that the federal government should promote U.S.-owned firms and should condition international investment in the United States on equivalent access to foreign markets. Such implications are reflected in the recent Office of Technology Assessment report, which proposes a specific reciprocity approach, affording equal treatment to investors according to mirror-image principles.

This concept of conditional national treatment has also been advanced in a series of recent reports by former U.S. Trade Representative negotiator Clyde Prestowitz and the Economic Strategy Institute (ESI).[15] A 1991 report on foreign investment charged that the Committee on Foreign Investment in the United States—the interagency group that reviews foreign acquisitions with national security implications—was too lenient and approved virtually everything that came its way. It raised the specter that control of key U.S. industries, from semiconductors to advanced materials, was slipping away to foreign competitors, and it made the case for stiffer performance requirements on foreign acquisitions of so-called sensitive U.S. companies.

A 1993 ESI study of the airline industry alleged that strategic investments by foreign airlines, such as British Airway's investment in USAir, were threatening the ability of American-owned airlines to gain access abroad, especially in Britain, and eroding the competitiveness of U.S.-owned airlines. And in a widely cited 1994 report on the United States and Europe, ESI contrasted investment from the European Community with that from Japan and Asia more broadly.

The study argued that while European-owned firms invest in ways that strengthen U.S. technology and production methods, Japanese- and Asian-owned companies invest strategically and in potentially damaging ways. The report thus made the case for differential treatment of investment by European and Japanese companies.

The framing of the debate in terms of what share of a corporation's assets is invested, what percentage of its activities take place in the United States, or worse yet, how its home government treats U.S.-owned firms is based on a shaky set of assumptions. Consider first the faulty logic of performance requirements. The balance of domestic-versus-international activities that such companies undertake cannot be determined by any legislatively mandated formula. The nature of this balance is likely to vary considerably between industrial sectors and fields of technology. Although automotive firms may be able to produce a large share of total content in the markets where products are sold, it will be much more difficult to achieve similar content in sectors like electronics, which are subject to much higher degrees of wage-related competition.

In other words, globalization affects all aspects of corporate strategy and behavior—technology, production, and markets. To be successful in an environment characterized by global markets, corporations must—and are frequently forced to—undertake both manufacturing and R&D on a global basis. R&D and innovation must take place in global centers of technology, whether in the United States, Europe, or Japan. Some forms of manufacturing have to take place near the markets, while others—particularly in highly priced competitive lines of business, where wages matter—have to take place in offshore locations.

From the perspective of domestic economic welfare, it is indeed advantageous when international companies like Honda or Sony decide to design, develop, and produce their products in the United States. It is also necessary for both U.S.- and foreign-owned companies to conduct a significant share of their activities outside the United States. Attempts to force foreign-owned or domestic firms in such industries to conduct higher shares of their activities in the United States, or to penalize them for holding offshore activities, are likely to have an adverse effect on the U.S. economy. Not only will such measures affect current investments, but also they are likely to make firms reluctant to undertake future investments as well, forfeiting millions, if not billions, of dollars in inflows.

It makes even less economic sense to penalize individual companies for the practices of their home-country governments. Such measures essentially impugn individual companies, regardless of their own record on investment, for governmental policies and practices they may not even support. Allegedly designed to open foreign markets, such measures run the risk of sparking foreign retaliation, thus poisoning the whole environment for foreign investment.

International Investment in a Globalizing Economy

Globalization and international cross-investment are the new and defining features of economic life. All aspects of corporate activity, from R&D and product development to production and marketing, must be oriented to and increasingly take place in major markets throughout the globe. Globalization is occurring through a variety of mechanisms, but none is more important than international investment, which has risen to all-time highs over the past decade. Federal legislation can provide little shelter from such pervasive globalization. Consider just a few facts. According to data compiled by the United Nations program on transnational corporations,[16] the world stock of international investment rose from $500 billion in 1980 to more than $2 trillion by 1992 (see table A–2). The pace was particularly dramatic between 1987 and 1992, when the amount of international investment doubled, a rate of growth that significantly exceeded that of trade.

The United States has been a primary beneficiary of this trend, as international investment has become the key mechanism through which the United States has integrated with the global economy. Indeed, the United States has been the recipient of a disproportionate share of the recent increase in international investment (see figure A–1). According to U.S. Department of Commerce data, inflows of international investment in the United States surged upward from $20 billion in 1985 to a peak of $68 billion in 1989 (see figure A–2).[17] This surge in investment was concentrated in the manufacturing sectors, as the international investment share of U.S. manufacturing doubled between 1985 and 1991. In fact, the United States—which for a long time was the world's largest outward investor—is now the largest recipient of inward investment as well. According to a recent Department of Commerce report:

> The internationalization of production by the world's largest corporations is a continuation of a process already underway in the late nineteenth century. In the 1950s and 1960s, the

rapid globalization of international production was led by many U.S.-owned firms and quickly followed en masse by international corporations. In the 1960s, U.S. outward direct investment grew rapidly, with U.S. firms accounting for about one-half of the world's direct investment outflows. By the 1980s, the U.S. was receiving about one-half of the world's direct investment inflows, reflecting the rapid rise in foreign firms' presence in the U.S. economy.[18]

By 1990, according to the Department of Commerce, there were 11,900 foreign-affiliated manufacturing establishments in the United States, employing 2.1 million manufacturing workers and having shipments in excess of $418 billion. International manufacturing investment was concentrated in the chemical, drug, computer, and consumer electronics industries (see table A–3). Foreign-affiliated manufacturers generated approximately $177 billion in value added, 13 percent of the value added by all U.S. manufacturing establishments. More than half the value added by foreign-owned manufacturing establishments was concentrated in four industries: chemicals and allied products ($49 billion), food products ($20 billion), electronics ($17 billion), and industrial equipment ($14 billion). International manufacturing investment in the United States came primarily from the advanced industrial nations, with just seven countries—Britain, Canada, Japan, Germany, France, Switzerland, and the Netherlands—accounting for more than 80 percent of the employment, shipments, and value added by foreign-affiliated manufacturers. British-owned establishments accounted for the largest share of production (23 percent), followed by Canadian-owned establishments (15 percent) and Japanese-owned establishments (13 percent).[19]

Although much as been made of so-called asymmetries in international investment, a review of the most current data available from the Department of Commerce suggests that this issue has been overblown. Such contentions, which are typically based on an analysis of short-term investment flows, are not borne out by longer-term trends. The notion that investment patterns between the United States and Japan are asymmetrical, for example, is based almost exclusively on the unique pattern of the mid-to-late 1980s, when Japan was building a production base in North America in response to both market and political pressures. In fact, investment flows from a given country vary greatly from year to year, reflecting economic conditions in the home country.

In recent years, international investment has shown a close relationship to the business cycle. When companies and nations grow, they invest abroad; but when hard times hit, investment slows. Throughout the late 1980s, it is indeed true that investment inflows into the United States exceeded the investments made by American companies abroad (see figure A–3). In 1989, for example, the United States posted a $32 billion investment gap with the rest of the world. This gap has narrowed considerably in recent years, however, as a result of the U.S. recovery and the Japanese and European recessions. Indeed, by 1993 the gap had turned into a sizable surplus, as U.S. investments of $58 billion abroad were more than $35 billion greater than foreign investments of $22.6 billion in America.[20]

This basic pattern holds for both Europe and Japan. In 1989, the United States posted an investment deficit with Europe of roughly $19 billion, as European companies invested $43 billion in the United States, while American companies invested $24 billion in Europe. But by 1992 this had turned into an investment surplus of more than $13 billion, as European investment in the United States fell to $800 million, while U.S. investment was $13.5 billion. The gap has closed for Japanese investment as well. In 1989, Japanese companies posted a $17 billion investment surplus with the United States, investing $18 billion in the United States, while U.S. companies invested $300 million in Japan. But by 1993, this surplus had narrowed to less than $1 billion, as U.S. companies invested $1.3 billion in Japan as compared with Japanese investments of $2.2 billion in the United States.[21]

Furthermore, while Congress is debating how to restrict international investment, it has failed to notice that international investment in the United States has declined and that investment on a global basis may be shifting away from North America and toward Asia. After increasing to some $68 billion in 1989, international investment in the United States plummeted to $11.5 billion in 1992, before rebounding to $22.6 billion in 1993.[22] In 1992 and 1993, Japanese investment in U.S. manufacturing dropped sharply, according to the U.S. Department of Commerce. Japanese investment in the United States plummeted from a high of more than $18.7 billion in 1988 to just $2.2 billion in 1993.[23] The falloff in Japanese investment is especially damaging since it was largely concentrated in manufacturing, particularly automobiles and steel. Indeed, Japanese investment has been redirected away from the United States and toward Asia, as the rapid appreciation of the yen has forced a shift to offshore production. According to Japan External Trade Organization (JETRO), Japanese investment in China is growing at a rate of 25 percent per year and continues to flow to the ASEAN countries, particularly Malaysia and Thailand, even as Japan remains mired in recession.[24] These nations are developing growth strategies premised on international investment.[25] European investment in the United States also fell, declining from a high of $43 billion in 1988 to near zero in 1992—a year when the United Kingdom, the Netherlands, France, and Italy all registered capital outflows from the United States. European investment, however, rebounded significantly to $27.5 billion in 1993, though this remains below massive inflows of European investment of the 1980s.

The New View of International Investment

A new view on investment has emerged in the past decade, largely in response to these trends. The classic view of international investment and of the multinational corporation is that the principal motive for international investment is the desire of multinational firms to secure the least costly production of goods for sale in world markets. According to this view, international direct investment in manufacturing is determined by the growth and strategies of oligopolistic corporations seeking to minimize costs—particularly labor costs—and maximize profits. Furthermore direct manufacturing investment revolves around sector-specific strategies and is usually based on significant advantages over local firms, which the international investors seek to preserve through location in areas that increase access to markets and reduce costs of production.[26]

The theory of international investment evolved in the late 1950s and the 1960s. It is based in large measure on the work of John Dunning in England, Raymond Vernon at Harvard, Charles Kindleberger at MIT, and especially Kindlebergers's student, Stephen Hymer. This theory rests upon two concepts: the product cycle and the international division of labor. The classic product cycle model advanced by Vernon shows that international investment occurs over the product's life cycle, with products initially introduced in the home market and later dispersed to offshore locations as they become mature and the manufacturing process becomes standardized.[27] The international division of labor approach associated with Hymer, among others, began with the notion that doing business abroad and managing an international network of operations involve considerable costs that can be offset only by substantial firm-specific advantages or assets, mainly in the form of economies of scale or superior technology.[28]

Hymer further suggested that multinational firms usually place the different aspects or stages of their activities in different locations throughout the globe. In other words, multinational corporations strategically arrange their activities according to an international division of labor, with high-level administration, finance, and technology development, for examples, occurring in central, core locations and more standard production and labor located in lower-wage, peripheral locations. More recent contributions from the field of industrial organization economics suggest that international investment reflects a particular type of firm-specific asset, referred to as an "internalization" advantage. Such an asset might be a particularly high level of quality, for example. This approach would make international investment the preferred way to enter foreign markets.[29] Oliver Williamson and David Teece similarly argue that international investment represents a way of overcoming significant transaction costs involved in trade and technology licensing arrangements.[30]

John Dunning has advanced his so-called eclectic paradigm, which combines the notions of firm-specific advantages, locational advantages, and internalization.[31] He suggests that international investments result when: (1) a firm has advantages such as technology or products that it can exploit in global markets; (2) overseas investment offers a cost-effective mechanism for exploiting such advantages, as for example if offshore production offers greater returns than technology licensing; or (3) overseas factor conditions are favorable. Michael Porter has argued that globalization is becoming a key element of corporate strategy, influenced by high degrees of international competition and the need to exploit both local and international factors of production, particularly clusters of related and supporting industries.[32]

By and large, the conventional theory suggests that international investment is driven by firms—for the most part oligopolistic ones— seeking to exploit advantages that come from economies of scale or superior technology to preserve or increase market share and reduce costs of production—particularly labor costs. Most of these advantages are reinforced by market failures, asymmetries in information, or high transaction costs in moving goods or services between nations. Interestingly, this view has done little to counter the popular notion that international investment generates costs and is at times injurious to host nations by generating dependence on foreign sources of technology, influencing a pattern of uneven development, and eroding the power of nation-states to control their own destinies.[33]

The new focus on international investment turns attention to the relationship between the globalization of production, international investment, and domestic productivity growth. It suggests that international investment is often the source of technology transfer, new management practices, and knowledge that leads to productivity improvements, employment growth, and increasing wealth for the host nation. This role should not be minimized.

Improving productivity is the major economic challenge facing the advanced industrial nations, and foreign direct investment will play a pivotal role in achieving that growth.[34] International investment in the form of transplant or foreign-owned manufacturing establishments increases competition in local markets, forcing all producers to improve their performance. Domestic producers benefit from the augmented competition, because these investors bring in international "best practices" to the domestic scene. Knowledge of such best practices spreads through imitation, as local firms become suppliers to transplants through joint ventures between transplants and domestic firms, through the regular flow of information between transplants and their local suppliers and clients, and through the normal rotation of personnel. The introduction of best practices by foreign investors results in a general rise of productivity levels in the domestic manufacturing base, setting in motion a "virtuous cycle" (as opposed to a vicious one) of imitation, adaptation, and improvement. Productivity improvements enable firms to generate more jobs and pay better salaries, increasing domestic income levels and creating more affluent and demanding local customers. These customers put pressure on companies to keep themselves active in the search for best practices in all areas of business and management, which in turn leads companies to increase their exposure to the demands of globalization and thereby to improve the ability of the domestic economy to attract additional foreign investment.

Transplants play a key role in productivity improvement by transferring both state-of-the-art technology and work organization to the countries in which they are located. A recent report on *Manufacturing Productivity* by the McKinsey Global Institute in conjunction with Robert Solow and Martin Baily focuses on nine key manufacturing sectors in the United States, Europe, and Japan, and provides striking evidence of the role of transplants in fostering productivity growth.[35] The McKinsey study found that these transplant factories have played a far more important role than trade in improving productivity in both the United States and Europe, noting that:

> Transplants from leading-edge producers: (1) directly contribute to higher levels of domestic productivity, (2) prove that leading-edge productivity can be achieved with local inputs, (3) put competitive pressure on other domestic producers, and (4) transfer knowledge of best-practices to other domestic producers through natural movement of personnel. Moreover, foreign direct investment has provoked less political opposition than trade because it creates jobs instead of destroying them. Thus, it is likely to grow faster in years to come.[36]

The McKinsey study confirms that these forces are universal, operating not only in the United States but also in the major industrial economies such as Japan and Germany. Figure A–6 provides a useful synthesis of the main findings. The horizontal axis on this figure is a productivity ranking, where 1 represents the highest attainable productivity level and 3 the lowest. The vertical axis classifies the types of competition to which firms are exposed into three categories: local, regional, and global. The analysis indicates a close relationship between productivity and the degree to which an industry is exposed to the forces of global competition. First, world class productivity is attained only by sectors that are exposed to global competition. Second, and contrary to the thrust of the conventional wisdom of the past few years, the United States attains top productivity rankings in several sectors, including traditional heavy manufacturing sectors—indeed, the same sectors that are typically seen as symbols of U.S. industrial decline.

The study offers a compelling explanation for the comparative performance of industrial sectors—one that provides important guidance for policy. The most competitive sectors were those that faced a high degree of global exposure, particularly through open international investment. U.S. sectors that were exposed to high degrees of competition through open policies toward both trade and investment scored consistently high. This is clear for automobiles and steel, which have high levels of international investment and the establishment of Japanese transplant factories. It is also clear for high-technology electronics, where U.S. semiconductor and computer manufacturers have responded to the test of global competition. In consumer electronics, Japanese and European producers have recreated a world-class manufacturing base on American soil. High levels of European investment and transplant factories in the chemical and pharmaceutical sectors have contributed to world-class U.S. productivity in these sectors as well.

The McKinsey study shows that European strategies that have sought to bolster domestic industries either through trade protection or by restricting inflows of foreign investment have backfired, as firms and industrial sectors with lower levels of global exposure have lagged badly behind those that have been forced to meet the tests of global competition at home and abroad. In fact, U.S. openness is a key source of economic advantage, vis-à-vis both Europe and Japan. The U.S. open investment regime is a source of global capital, technology, and management practices that have created a truly globalized, state-of-the-art, high-productivity industrial base—a source of considerable advantage in an increasingly global economy.

A recently completed OECD study provides additional evidence of the link connecting international investment, productivity, and economic growth. Comparing investment and productivity patterns in fifteen advanced industrial nations, the OECD study found that foreign-owned companies are typically more efficient than domestic firms both in absolute levels and in rates of productivity growth. The study found that these productivity gains resulted from the foreign-owned companies' using more advanced technology than that used by domestic industries, or from adding capacity. By contrast, productivity increases at locally owned companies more often resulted from downsizing and layoffs.

The study also found that international investment has been a key source of employment growth across the advanced industrial nations. In ten of fifteen nations studied, foreign-owned companies generated new employment more rapidly than did their domestically owned counterparts, sometimes expanding their operations while domestic firms were contracting. In three others they eliminated jobs, but they did so more slowly than did domestically owned enterprises. The largest employment declines occurred in Japan and Germany, where soaring costs during the 1980s caused international investors to cut a significant number of jobs. Interestingly, employment at U.S. subsidiaries in Japan fell by roughly 30 percent over the course of the 1980s. This supports the view that investment differentials between the United States and Japan—particularly the considerable differentials of the 1980s—are not simply the result of formal and informal barriers but rather reflect considerable market dynamics as well.[37] Furthermore, the OECD study points to a link between investment and trade, as foreign subsidiaries tend to export and import more than domestic firms, with most of the imports taking the form of intrafirm trade.

The Evidence on Foreign Investment and the United States

This virtuous-cycle view of foreign investment clashes with that of some leading individuals in the policy debate, who view foreign investment as a zero-sum game of "us versus them." But the evidence is overwhelmingly on the side of the positive-sum view investment illustrated in figure A–4. A review of the available evidence demonstrates, for example, that foreign investment strengthens the American economy, stimulates investment, improves productivity, generates jobs, and helps to position firms and regions for success in a rapidly globalizing economy.

   The preponderance of available evidence indicates that international investment in U.S. manufacturing has generated productivity increases and value-added significantly greater than American-owned manufacturing has generated (see figure A–5). Productivity grew more rapidly in manufacturing establishments of international affiliates in the United States than for the manufacturing sector as a whole during the 1980s. In real terms, the gross product of international affiliates rose nearly four times as fast as for all manufacturing establishments between 1980 and 1987. According to Department of Commerce data, labor productivity in manufacturing industries, measured as value added per production employee, was nearly 30 percent higher for foreign-owned establishments than for U.S.-owned establishments—$74 per hour, as compared with $52 per hour. The Department of Commerce analysis further indicates that the productivity of foreign-owned establishments was higher than that of U.S.-owned establishments in a significant number of industries; it was more than 10 percent higher in 153 of the 312 industries examined. The productivity of foreign-owned establishments was lower than that of U.S.-owned establishments in considerably fewer industries. According to the Department of Commerce data, it was at least 10 percent lower in just

70 industries. In 89 industries, foreign-owned establishments had productivity that was roughly equal to that of U.S.-owned establishments.[38] The Department of Commerce analysis suggests that these productivity differentials reflect the tendency for foreign-owned establishments to be concentrated in industries in which productivity is high, and they stemmed from the higher levels of plant size, capital intensity, and employee skill found in foreign-owned manufacturing establishments rather than from foreign ownership per se.

International investors have invested more in plant and equipment over the past few years than have their domestic counterparts. Department of Commerce data show that in 1988, international affiliates spent almost 50 percent more on plant and equipment per worker than the average for all U.S. manufacturing.[39]

These data further indicate that during the past few years, plant and equipment expenditures by international affiliates increased much more rapidly than did such expenditures by U.S.-owned businesses. From 1987 to 1990, for example, the rate of increase in plant-and-equipment expenditures for international affiliates (for example, nonbank, nonagricultural business) was five times greater than that for U.S.-owned business, 106 percent versus 21 percent. Between 1987 and 1990, Japanese-owned enterprises had a far higher rate of increase in new plant and equipment spending (up by 157 percent) than had any other major foreign ownership group. The largest percentage increases in new plant and equipment spending between 1987 and 1990 occurred in automotive-related industries, where major new Japanese investments were concentrated. European companies also invested heavily in U.S. plant and equipment. In 1990 alone, U.S. subsidiaries of European firms invested more than $38 billion in modernizing and upgrading their American facilities. As a whole, European-owned companies spend more on new plant and equipment than do U.S. manufacturing businesses. Foreign firms in general invested roughly 45 percent more than their U.S. counterparts—$12,200 versus $8,400 per employee in 1988, with nearly half the capital payments of foreign firms in the United States made by European firms.[40]

Interestingly, by helping to improve productivity and to bolster the performance of domestic industry, international investment has contributed to the expansion of trade and the export-driven economic turnaround of the late 1980s and early 1990s that restored the United States to its position as the world's largest exporter. Exports by international affiliates increased from $52 billion in 1980 to $98 billion, or 23 percent of total U.S. exports, in 1990. Manufacturing exports by international affiliates grew from $9 billion in 1980 to more than $32 billion in 1990. This link between foreign direct investment and trade is enhanced by alliances and supply relationships between foreign-owned and domestic companies, which help U.S. companies to gain inroads into foreign markets.

The Role of Transplants. Transplant factories have played a key role in the revitalization of American industry, accelerating the adoption and diffusion of new methods of production organization. Transplants have shown that new forms of production and work organization, such as teams, rotation of workers from task to task, quality control circles, and continuous improvement schedules can work in American industry with American workers.

Other evidence supports the view that transplants have played a key role in bolstering U.S. productivity through the transfer of new management methods and practices. Research conducted in collaboration with Martin Kenney identifies a high rate of adoption and diffusion of new organizational practices among automotive-related transplants. As table A–4 shows, our 1988 survey of the entire population of Japanese transplant automotive parts suppliers found that more than three-quarters of them organized work in production teams; 71 percent used teams self-directed by workers; 82 percent rotated workers within these teams; 62 percent rotated workers between teams; 44 percent made use of quality circles where teams of workers engage in efforts to improve quality; and nearly 75 percent planned to use quality circles in the future.[41.]

The adoption and diffusion of these management practices at Japanese automotive-related transplants are significantly higher than for U.S. manufacturing as a whole. According to a 1993 survey conducted by Paul Osterman of a random sample of roughly 800 U.S. manufacturing establishments, roughly 50 percent of U.S. manufacturing plants report the use of teams, 55 percent rotate workers between teams, and 45 percent report the use of quality circles.[42] My own field research and interviews indicate that these practices are taking root in many of the steel joint ventures as well. At LSE, the LTV-Sumitomo joint venture in Cleveland, and at I/N Tek, a joint venture between Inland Steel and Nippon Steel, management and labor have agreed to implement new work systems that reduced job classifications to a minimum, removed front-line supervisors, structured work in teams, and empowered workers to engage in continuous improvement and make decisions typically reserved for management.[43]

Transplants have also helped to facilitate the diffusion of state-of-the-art management practices into the U.S. industrial base. Many transplants, particularly those in the automotive industry, work with their suppliers to help them adopt these world-class practices. Our detailed research at transplant factories indicates that Toyota and Honda have set up supplier-support programs to encourage and facilitate the adoption of world-class practices among their suppliers. A growing number of domestic suppliers are adopting these practices. Johnson Controls, for example, has adopted the Toyota Production System in its Kentucky factory, which supplies Toyota's Georgetown, Kentucky, facility. A just-in-time supplier, it begins producing seats for Camrys just as those Camrys start their way down Toyota's line. Johnson Controls has gotten Toyota business throughout North America and in Europe as well. The Kentucky facility is now a model both for Toyota suppliers in the United States and for other Johnson Controls plants around the world—diffusing these best practices back into the U.S. industrial base. Transplants have thus played a significant role in catalyzing the organizational transformation of the U.S. economy.

R&D and Technology. International investments have added to U.S. investment in R&D, significantly strengthening our technology base. There are now roughly 390 international research, product development, and design centers in the United States, providing more than $11 billion per year in R&D funding (see figures A–7 and A–8).[44]

European companies account for more than half of all U.S. R&D spending in industrial chemicals and more than 40 percent in the drug industry, strengthening U.S. technological capabilities in these areas and in the related field of biotechnology—industries where the United States remains at the forefront of global competition. Interviews with the executives in charge of these laboratories indicate that there are two main reasons why international corporations are locating R&D in the United States. The first is to achieve a higher degree of "global localization" by conducting R&D, factory production, and particularly product design and development all together in proximity to "foreign" markets. The second is to gain access to the pool of scientific and technical talent in established U.S. centers of technology and innovation.

R&D spending by international investors accounts for a rapidly rising share of the total R&D being performed in the United States. R&D spending by international affiliates grew from $6.5 billion in 1987 to $11.3 billion in 1990, an increase of nearly 75 percent. This compares with an increase of just 30 percent for U.S.-owned firms. International R&D spending also accounts for a growing share of the total U.S. technology base. According to the Department of Commerce, international affiliates provided roughly 15 percent of total R&D in the manufacturing sector in 1990, up from just 5.7 percent in 1980. Furthermore, international affiliates devote roughly 2.5 percent of sales to R&D and 6.5 percent of value addition—comparable to the spending done by U.S.-owned firms.

R&D spending by international affiliates is concentrated in those sectors where international companies lead rather than lag behind the United States—European companies in chemicals and drugs, Japanese and German companies in automotive-related technologies and consumer electronics. European R&D spending in the United States represents more than half (59 percent) of domestic R&D spending in industrial chemicals and synthetic materials. International R&D spending accounts for 42 percent of total R&D spending in the drug industry.[45] European firms make important contributions to the U.S. R&D base in chemicals and in medical and environmental technology.[46] This high level of foreign R&D and technology investment provides a potentially powerful explanation for the competitive strength of the U.S. chemical and pharmaceutical sectors.

Critics of international investment have suggested that such investment in R&D threatens U.S. technological leadership by giving international companies easy access to U.S. technology. Some have gone so far as to argue that foreign R&D facilities are merely listening posts whose main objective is to steal U.S. ideas and technology. Recent data compiled by the U.S. government and other sources suggest that this simply is not the case, since the net flow of R&D appears to be positive for the United States, according to several indicators. In fact, an analysis of royalty and license data conducted by the Department of Commerce found an overwhelmingly large net inflow of technology to U.S. affiliates from their foreign parents (see figures A–9 and A–10).

This analysis shows that net payments by U.S. affiliates to their foreign parents increased from $378 million in 1980 to $2.1 billion in 1991, and that payments by high-technology affiliates represent more than one-half of total payments by U.S. affiliates in the manufacturing and services sectors to foreign parents. It also found that British, German, and Japanese multinationals accounted for approximately 60 percent of total royalties and license-fee payments in high-technology industries. These patterns led the Department of Commerce to conclude: "The growing deficit of affiliates' payments over their receipts suggests that foreign parents are transferring more technology to their affiliates in the United States than the reverse."[47]

Employment and Jobs. President Clinton has pledged that his administration will take the high road to economic revitalization—placing emphasis on the creation of high-wage jobs with good benefits and security. The evidence suggests that international investors are already helping the U.S. economy move toward this high-road strategy.

International affiliates have generated good jobs at good wages throughout the nation. These affiliates also provide jobs for 4.7 million American workers, up from roughly 2 million in 1980. The jobs generated by international affiliates are heavily concentrated in the manufacturing sector, which accounts for roughly 2.1 million jobs (see figure A–11; also see table A–5). European transplants accounted for 1.3 million manufacturing jobs, while Japanese transplants provided roughly 300,000 manufacturing in 1990. International affiliates account for 5 percent of all U.S. employment but employ 10.9 percent of all Americans in the manufacturing sector. Employment in foreign affiliates made up more than 10 percent of total U.S. employment in the following sectors: chemicals; petroleum and coal; stone, clay, and glass; primary metals; electronics; rubber; instruments; food processing; and industrial machinery.

Furthermore, Department of Commerce data indicate that international affiliates are concentrated in capital-intensive manufacturing industries and in those that require a higher level of employee skill. According to data released in October 1993 by the Department of Commerce, more than 85 percent of the work force in Japanese automotive transplants are engaged in production jobs, in comparison with just 60 percent for all manufacturing establishments in that industry.

These statistics have not precluded the rise of a significant debate over the employment impacts of international investment. Several authors have argued that foreign investment in the automotive industry has had a damaging effect on U.S. manufacturing and workers. A large part of the debate has been centered on the employment effects of the Japanese automotive transplants, with several studies arguing that Japanese investment in the automotive sector has displaced jobs provided by domestic producers. A 1989 study by Norman Glickman and Douglas Woodward argued that international investment tends to displace more jobs than it creates.[48] In 1988, the U.S. General Accounting Office (GAO) estimated that the automotive transplants would create 112,000 new jobs and displace 156,000 jobs between 1985 and 1990, resulting in a net job loss of roughly 44,000 jobs.[49] In a follow-up study done in 1989, the GAO estimated that Japanese automobile-related production in the United States provided 66,000 jobs but displaced 77,000 other jobs, resulting in a net job loss of 11,000 jobs.[50] A United Auto Workers study estimated a net job loss of between 74,000 and 194,000 jobs over the same period.[51] A recent study published by the Economic Policy Institute suggests that the recent influx of Japanese automotive transplants has resulted in the displacement of jobs provided by the traditional Big Three automotive manufacturers, and a reduction in the total wage and benefit levels provided to workers in this industry.[52]

These conclusions have to be approached cautiously. The problem is that these studies assume a causal relationship between transplants and the performance of domestic firms. This assumption neglects the fact that domestic firms face competition not only from transplants but also from domestically owned and global rivals producing in other markets. Simply put, the real issue is not transplants versus domestic producers. U.S. jobs may have been lost anyway as a result of foreign competition.

Indeed, transplant production has clearly offset import penetration, trading offshore jobs for domestic ones. Evidence confirming this substitution effect is abundant. A February 1991 report in *Ward's Auto World* indicated that in 1986, imports accounted for 28.3 percent of total U.S. vehicle sales, while exports accounted for just 4.7 percent. By 1990, however, imports had decreased to 25.8 percent, while transplant production accounted for 15.2 percent. Remarkably, by 1991, Japanese car makers were holding back exports to protect their U.S. production facilities and retain jobs for American workers.[53] A recent report in *Business Week* citing data collected by Autofacts Inc. indicates that four Japanese auto makers—Honda, Toyota, Mitsubishi, and Nissan—have reached the point where more than half the cars they sell in the United States are made in North America. This is a substantial improvement over the situation just two years ago, when only Honda could make that claim.[54]

The real issue is strikingly simple: Do we want the jobs, or alternatively, would we prefer them to stay in factories in other countries that ship their products to our shores? Our database of more than 350 automotive-related transplants indicates that the employment provided by these Japanese transplants accounts for approximately 110,000 direct jobs, excluding any indirect multiplier effects (see table A–6). This estimate is conservative, counting only those establishments that have majority-Japanese ownership.

Moreover, from a macroeconomic perspective, the entire issue of displacement is moot, since attempts to calculate employment impacts by sector represent a fundamental misreading of the issue. In reviewing the evidence, Edward Graham and Paul Krugman note: "The net impact of FDI on U.S. employment is approximately zero, and the truth of this assertion has nothing to do with job gains and losses at the industry level."[55] The reason, they assert, "has nothing to do with the results of the job effects at the regional or industry level, but rests on the macroeconomic point that employment in the United States is essentially determined by supply, not demand, except in the very short run."

Wages and Compensation. International affiliates also pay higher-than-average compensation and wages. Annual compensation levels in foreign-owned manufacturing establishments were approximately $5,300 higher than those for U.S.-owned establishments in 1990— $38,300, as compared with $33,000.[56] Furthermore, the Department of Commerce analysis shows that compensation per employee in foreign-owned establishments was more than 10 percent higher than that of U.S.-owned establishments in 131 of 312 industries examined, whereas it was more than 10 percent lower in just 28 industries. As figure A–12 indicates, international affiliates and U.S. establishments pay comparable rates across a wide range of industrial sectors.

In terms of production workers, foreign-owned manufacturing establishments pay higher average hourly wages than do U.S.-owned manufacturers. The average hourly wage for production workers in foreign-owned manufacturing establishments was 12 percent higher than that for U.S.-owned manufacturers—$12.57, as compared with $11.04 per hour. Comparing the wages of production workers is a particularly useful exercise, because it provides some level of control for occupational mixtures, eliminating variations in the ratio of production workers to other workers as a source of differences in pay. Furthermore, production workers constitute a relatively homogeneous group, particularly in comparison with other workers who may represent a wide variety of occupations.

The Department of Commerce analysis further indicates that the wages of production workers were more than 10 percent higher in foreign-owned establishments than in U.S.-owned establishments in 113 of the 312 industries examined, whereas they were at least 10 percent lower in only 43 industries. Interestingly, five of the industries in which the wage rates of foreign-owned establishments were significantly lower than those of U.S.-owned establishments were automotive-related. The Department of Commerce analysis notes that the lower wage rates in these industries may reflect the fact that these plants are recent establishments and have a work force with less accumulated job tenure than have typical U.S.-owned establishments. Industry data indicate, however, that Japanese automotive assembly transplants pay relatively high wages, which are more or less on par with those provided by Big Three producers (see table A–7).

Labor-Management Relations. International investment demonstrates that labor and management can work together to institute cooperative relations, establish cutting-edge work practices, improve productivity, and retain and create jobs. Many have argued that international investment works against unions. A detailed econometric analysis of the factors that shaped the location decisions of more than 1,000 Japanese transplants, conducted jointly with Donald Smith, shatters the myths that Japanese transplants avoid unions, high-wage urban areas, or places with relatively high concentrations of minority populations.[57] In fact, our analysis indicates that Japanese companies in the automotive sector prefer to locate in relatively high-wage, unionized, densely manufacturing areas, rather than in rural areas. The most important factors were proximity to a large Japanese assembly facility and location in an area with a well-developed and specialized manufacturing base.

Related research conducted in collaboration with Martin Kenney shows that international investors, particularly Japanese investors, have formed successful alliances between business and labor, helping to provide models of constructive and cooperative labor-management partnerships from which U.S. industry and management are learning. National Steel, which is 70 percent owned by NKK, has established a new cooperative partnership with the United Steel Workers Union, which not only has resulted in better and more constructive relations but also has allowed management to reduce the number of job classifications and introduce new technology, resulting in considerable productivity increases. Workers and their unions were able to buy into this partnership because National Steel provided a guarantee that workers would not be laid off. Pioneering labor-management efforts that reduce the number of job classifications and organize work in teams have been implemented at a host of joint-venture steel transplants, including I/N Tek, the Inland Steel-Nippon Steel joint venture in Indiana; LSE, the LTV-Sumitomo Metal joint venture in Cleveland, Ohio; and Wheeling-Nisshin, the joint venture between Wheeling-Pittsburgh Steel and Nisshin Steel in West Virginia.[58] At the automotive transplants NUMMI and Diamond Star, management engaged the UAW in similarly constructive partnerships, reducing job classifications from the one hundred-plus norm to just three or four, implementing teams, and reducing work rules in return for good wages and increased job security.

Local Content. Foreign investment in the United States, it is often claimed, takes the form of low-end branch plants. The empirical evidence, however, does not support this statement. In their review of the evidence, Graham and Krugman note that the "data do not provide any support for the view that foreign firms typically keep the good jobs and high value-added activities at home."[59]

Many contend, however, that Japanese automotive transplants are a special case because the transplants simply do low value-added assembly work in the United States, keeping R&D and technology development at home and deriving their key components from Japan. According to this interpretation, these plants assemble cars from knocked-down kits imported from Japan, and they thus have a minimal impact on local and regional economic development. A related line of reasoning, referred to as the screwdriver hypothesis, is that Japanese plants have moved only standard, low value-added operations to the United States, keeping higher value-added, more sophisticated activities in Japan. The available evidence contradicts the screwdriver hypothesis. The automotive transplants produce high value-added components like engines and transmissions in the United States.[60] They also operate twenty-two R&D, product development, and design centers in the United States that design and develop cars for the North American and world markets (see table A–8).

Additionally at issue is the local content of the transplants. It is commonly asserted that the transplants derive more than half their parts from Japan; recent evidence, however, suggests that this is erroneous. A 1989 UAW study using foreign-merchandise imports as a measure of imported content concluded that transplants have low rates of domestic content. Not surprisingly, the study found that in 1988, foreign merchandise imports made up 61 percent of total merchandise at Mazda and 39 percent at Honda.[61]

Foreign-merchandise imports, however, do not provide an appropriate measure of foreign and domestic content. Domestic content refers to the direct material inputs such as steel, rubber, automotive parts, engines, and transmissions that are used in the manufacture and assembly of automobiles. Foreign-merchandise imports, however, include expensive capital equipment in the form of heavy machinery, machine tools, conveyor belts, and the assembly line itself. Mazda's 61 percent foreign-merchandise imports (reported in the UAW study) thus reflect the value of Japanese equipment imported during the plant's construction and start up in 1987–1988, not the actual components of each vehicle. While the transplants obtain a large share of dedicated capital equipment from Japan, they derive the bulk of in-process materials from the United States. Foreign-merchandise imports have declined lately, as transplant producers have completed initial start up and as capital equipment makers open more U.S. factories.

As table A–9 shows, domestic content has risen to between 65 and 75 percent for most transplant assembly plants. A survey of transplants suppliers done in 1988 reported a local content of 64 percent, a figure that has doubtless risen since then.[62] The increase in local content is attributable to three factors: (1) the movement of engine and transmission facilities to the United States; (2) the influx of Japanese automotive component suppliers, steel firms, and rubber plants; and (3) recent efforts by transplants to integrate U.S. suppliers.

Rustbelt Reindustrialization. A decade or two ago, numerous commentators predicted a shift of manufacturing investment and activity away from the U.S. industrial heartland to newer, lower-wage regions of the Sunbelt, Latin America, or Asia. These prophets of doom portrayed the future as one of deindustrialization and abandonment of industrial centers in the United States and Europe. The events of the past decade have shown such predictions to be incorrect. In fact, international investment has played a key role in the reindustrialization of America's so-called Rust Belt during the past decade. This investment came from two sources: from international companies, particularly Japanese companies, setting up facilities in the industrial Midwest, and also from the domestic companies that had to compete against these new participants in the U.S. economy.

Japanese investors have played a key role in this transformation. Japanese companies alone have invested more than $25 billion in eight major automotive assembly complexes, more than seventy joint-venture steel facilities, more than twenty rubber and tire factories, and roughly 400 automotive parts suppliers.[63] More than half this investment is concentrated in four Great Lakes states—Ohio, Indiana, Michigan, and Illinois (see figure A–13). These transplants have brought a significant influx of capital and world-class manufacturing technologies and organizational practices to the region. Honda's assembly complex in Marysville, Ohio, for example, has provided more than $2 billion in investment and created more than 10,000 jobs.

The transplants have shown that the combination of lean production techniques and American workers can yield productivity levels comparable to those of Japan. Japanese investment has also provided capital, technology, and organizational know-how that have helped to revitalize the region's steel industry. Japanese steel makers have invested billions of dollars in state-of-the-art steel finishing facilities throughout the region, and they have entered into joint ventures with the region's key integrated steel producers (see table A–10).[64] Furthermore, the combined investments of Japanese and European electronics companies have helped to rebuild the television production infrastructure of the region (see figure A–14). A key economic advantage of the region lies in its ability to attract a growing constellation of the world's best companies.

Transplant investment has helped to spur the adoption and diffusion of improved technology and organizational practice throughout the region. It has done so by placing competitive pressure on domestic competitors like Ford, Chrysler, and Goodyear and through a process of learning and adaptation on the part of domestic suppliers. The findings of a survey of roughly 200 Midwestern manufacturers we conducted in collaboration with the Council of Great Lakes Governors in 1993 indicate that roughly half the region's manufacturing base is engaged in the transformation to best-practice manufacturing management. More than half the firms responding to the survey have implemented production teams, roughly half have implemented total quality management programs, 55 percent use statistical process control, and 46 have instituted just-in-time systems for inventory control.

Today the industrial Midwest is a vibrant economic area of the country, thanks to foreign investment. Our analysis shows[65] that after a severe contraction from 1977 to 1987, manufacturing output in this part of the country grew 7.8 percent from 1987 to 1988, surpassing not only the 7.4 percent growth rate of the United States as a whole, but also the 6.3 percent rate for Japan and the 5.2 percent rate for Germany. From 1980 to 1988, manufacturing productivity in the new industrial heartland rose by 36 percent, as compared with 15 percent for Germany, 32 percent for the United States, and 52 percent for Japan.

Roughly 15 percent of this gain for the region came from 1986 to 1988, a surge that even the Japanese economy could not match. A Federal Reserve Bank of Chicago study found Midwestern manufacturers to be 20 percent more efficient than their national counterparts. Furthermore, the Chicago Fed found that capital expenditure per worker was 9 percent higher in the Midwest from 1986 to 1990 than for the rest of the nation. Investment per worker was 16 percent higher in the Midwest transportation sector and 22 percent higher in the region's steel industry.[66]

Meanwhile, manufacturing employment has virtually stabilized. Despite having only 30 percent of the nation's population, the region accounts for 36 percent of all manufacturing output in the United States, 60 percent of the steel, 55 percent of the automobiles, and 50 percent of the machine tools. Remarkably, the industrial heartland produced more automobiles and steel in 1992 than a decade before, even after counting the General Motors plant closings. The Midwestern manufacturing belt was largely spared in the bicoastal recession of the early 1990s. In a striking reversal of regional economic fortunes, regions and states like New England, the Sunbelt, New York, and even California, which led the nation in growth through the mid-1980s, remain mired in recession, while once written-off areas of the industrial heartland are going strong.

Battle Creek, Michigan, provides a striking illustration of the role of international investment in regional economic transformation.[67] During the late 1960s and 1970s, Battle Creek was synonymous with deindustrialization, as its manufacturing base of food and cereal producers, agricultural equipment factories, and automotive parts producers experienced severe disinvestment and a wave of plant closings. In 1968, the U.S. government closed Fort Custer, eliminating thousands of jobs and causing closings of a host of defense-related businesses. Moreover, the manufacturing shakeout and deindustrialization crisis that occurred from the mid-1970s through the early 1980s had a calamitous effect on the local economy. Automobile parts and farm machinery factories closed down, and by the early 1980s, unemployment was over 20 percent.

The city responded with a coordinated strategy to rebuild itself by attracting high-performance companies from around the world and by developing an explicit strategy for using international investment as a vehicle for economic revitalization. After converting the abandoned Fort Custer military base into an industrial park, Battle Creek is currently home to roughly a dozen Japanese automotive parts companies and other manufacturing firms, employing approximately 2,000 workers. In fact, it now has the single largest concentration of transplant automotive-parts producers in the United States. Anchoring this Japanese manufacturing complex is a $200 million Nippondenso factory that produces air conditioners, heaters, condensers, and electrical parts for Toyota, Mazda, Honda, Mitsubishi, SIA, and the Big Three. In close proximity are three related suppliers that supply Nippondenso on a just-in-time basis: Koyo Metals, Tokai Rika, and Toyota Tsusho. Rounding out the complex are other Japanese firms: Hi-Lex, the former Nippon Cable Company; I.I. Stanley, a Honda supplier; and Technical Auto Parts, which makes suspension systems for Honda and Ford.

Battle Creek created a new nonprofit agency, Battle Creek Unlimited, to manage the industrial park, established a foreign trade zone and inland port, and opened an office in Tokyo. The city is now developing new approaches to worker training and vocational education to train workers to meet the needs of the new economy. In this regard, the Battle Creek strategy provides a useful guide for regional development policy, because it focuses on creating and strengthening value-added assets—providing services and infrastructure that enhance the potential for economic and industrial development, as opposed to the more conventional practice of luring companies with large financial incentives.

Toward a Multilateral Investment Agenda

America's policy toward international investment is clearly headed in a restrictionist direction. This is unfortunate. The current congressional drift toward restriction—whether in the form of conditional national treatment or performance requirements—is counterproductive for both the domestic and the global economies. Worse yet, it runs counter to the fundamental forces at work in the world economy.

The overwhelming weight of the evidence indicates that international investment generates substantial benefits for the U.S. economy. International investment is a key source of productivity improvement and economic growth. Over the course of the past decade, international investment has proved to be a more effective vehicle for bolstering the U.S. economy than government bailouts or federal subsidies for so-called critical technologies. International investment has also proved to be a much better mechanism for stimulating exports than agreements that force foreign countries to buy American products.

An open international investment policy therefore has much to offer the U.S. economy. The United States must reaffirm its long-standing commitment to investment and the equal treatment of all investors. Policy makers must reject recent initiatives that invoke national security as the reason for new restrictions on international investment. They must also resist the temptation to make international investment a vehicle for opening foreign markets or for penalizing international investors for the problematic actions of their governments.

This nation must continue to pursue a multilateral set of rules on investment. By itself, the United States is ill equipped to deal with the extraordinary rise of international investment and the onset of an increasingly integrated international economic order. It is simply beyond the capacity of any nation-state to deal with the global investment explosion that has outpaced the existing international legal framework. A new round of multilateral policy making and institution building will be required to create new rules and regulations for investment on a global scale. The time has come for a truly multilateral approach to investment—a GATT-like agreement—that would remove legal impediments to cross-border investments and would ensure that all nations treat foreign companies as they treat domestic ones. Such a general agreement on investment is a logical extension of the GATT, and is just as valuable for building a prosperous global economy.

The OECD has already moved to develop such a framework.[68] In March 1993, the OECD ministers called for a feasibility study of a wider investment instrument, and in August of that year a working group on this issue completed its initial report for consideration by

the Committee on International Investment and Multinational Enterprises, and ultimately by the OECD ministers. The OECD study
highlighted the fact that increasing protectionism and reciprocity
requirements threaten the free flow of investment, noting that
"despite the fact that FDI far outstripped growth in international
trade, there is no comprehensive multilateral investment instrument
underlying foreign investment." It concluded that existing multilateral arrangements such as the World Bank Guidelines on Investment
lack the muscle required to deal with the growth of investment and
do not even go as far as existing bilateral investment treaties and
regional arrangements on investment such as the NAFTA. It thus
called for a legally binding agreement that "by virtue of its treaty sta-
tus would be given more weight by the international community and
would also serve to directly engage Member countries' legislatures."
Such an agreement could pave the way for better international
investment conditions by eliminating existing restrictions and providing increased investment liberalization for all participants in the
international economy.

The OECD's proposal would seek to provide legally binding
obligations on all OECD members at all levels of government. It
would thus put more teeth into the already existing OECD Liberalization Codes and the National Treatment Instrument. The main purpose of the OECD instrument would be to achieve a greater level of
liberalization by improving the existing instruments and removing
obstacles to the establishment of competitive opportunities for foreign investors. The instruments would initially apply to the OECD
nations, which account for the great bulk of international cross-
investment, but could be extended to include non-OECD members as
well. The OECD instrument would also provide for clear definitions
of international investment and provisions for investment protection,
expropriation, and compensation. The OECD has already outlined a
number of alternatives for achieving such a multilateral agreement
on investment. While the OECD report notes that numerous business
groups and some labor federations have expressed support for such a
multilateral agreement, it remains up to the multinational business
community and the advanced industrial nations to do the hard work
of bringing such a framework into being. Such an agreement is clearly both a logical and a necessary extension of the Uruguay Round.

International investment has already done much to increase
productivity, by creating good jobs, advancing new technologies, and

most important, stimulating a powerful transformation to world-class, best-practice management in America. That is why American policy makers must embrace international investment as a centerpiece of a new global economic agenda for the United States. And that is why they must work together with other nations to create a new international legal and policy framework for investment that is in sync with the emerging global economic order.

Tables and Figures

TABLE A–1
Conditional National Treatment Legislation, 1974–1993

Law	Eligibility Restrictions for Program Participants
Stevenson-Wydler Technology Innovation Act of 1980 (as amended by Technology Transfer Act, Advanced Technology Program Acts)	Home government of foreign parties must permit U.S. persons to enter into Cooperative Research and Development Agreements (CRADAs) and licensing agreements
American Technology Preeminence Act, including the Technology Administration Authorization Act of 1991 (P.L. 102-45)	Home country of foreign-owned firm must afford U.S.-owned companies:
Advanced Technology Program (ATP)	1. opportunities comparable to those afforded to any other company to participate in joint ventures similar to those authorized under ATP
	2. local investment opportunites
	3. "adequate and effective" protection for intellectual property rights of U.S.-owned companies
Energy Policy Act of 1992	ATP conditions[a]
Defense Authorization Legislation of 1992	ATP conditions[a]
National Cooperative Production Amendments of 1993	Foreign-owned company's parent country must grant "national treatment" to U.S. companies in its national competition law covering joint ventures[b]

Proposals[c]	Eligibility Restrictions for Program Participants
Energy Labs Bill (S. 473) (amended by Rep. Sharp, May 1994)	For CRADAs with Department of Energy Labs ATP conditions[a]
Amendments to the Trade Act of 1974 (H.R. 249) (introduced January 5, 1993)	Actions by a foreign country denying national treatment in investment may be actionable under Section 301.
National Competitiveness Act of 1993 (H.R. 820) (introduced February 1993) Department of Commerce and National Science Foundation programs Manton amendment	Home government of the foreign-owned firm must: 1. provide U.S. companies "comparable" opportunities and offer them "access to resources and information equivalent to opportunities authorized under this legislation 2. have "open and transparent standards-setting process that results in standards that are fair and reasonable" 3. meet the second and third ATP conditions (Senate companion(S.4) does not contain this Manton amendment)
Aeronautical Technology Consortium Act of 1993 (S. 419/H.R. 1675) (introduced February 24, 1993, and April 2, 1993)	Home country of foreign-owned firm must 1. afford U.S.-owned companies opportunities comparable to those afforded any other company in R&D consortiums to which government of that country provides funding directly or indirectly through international organizations or agreements 2. afford "adequate and effective" protection for intellectual property rights of U.S.-owned companies
Hydrogen Future Act of 1993 (H.R. 1479) (introduced March 25, 1993)	Restricted to U.S.-owned firms
National Environmental Technology Act of 1993 (S. 978) (introduced May 18, 1993)	ATP conditions[a]

(Table continues)

TABLE A–1 (continued)

Proposals[c]	Eligibility Restrictions for Program Participants
National Aeronautics and Space Administration Act (S. 1881) (introduced March 1, 1994)	ATP conditions[a]
Omnibus Space Commercialization Act of 1993 (H.R. 2731) (introduced July 23, 1993)	ATP conditions[a]
Fair Trade in Financial Services Act of 1993 (S. 1527) (introduced October 7, 1993)	Authorizes sanctions against firms from countries that deny national treatment to U.S. financial services firms
Fair Trade in Services Act of 1993 (H.R. 3565) (introduced November 19, 1993)	Authorizes sanctions against foreign governments restricting U.S. firms in telecommunications and financial services
Authorizations for the Earthquake Hazards Reduction Act of 1977 (H.R. 3485) (introduced November 10, 1993)	No contract or subcontract can be made with a company organized under laws of a foreign country unless that country affords comparable opportunities to U.S. companies[b]
Hazardous Materials Transportation Act Amendments of 1993 (H.R. 2178) (passed by House November 21, 1993)	Waives mandatory filing requirement for persons not domiciled in U.S. if the country where person is domiciled does not require a U.S. domiciliary to file registration statements for same purpose; also contains ATP conditions[a]

a. Contains reciprocity conditions and language identical or similar to that for the Advanced Technology Program.
b. Rule may be waived if it violates GATT or any international agreement.
c. Unless noted otherwise, language is as originally introduced. CNT bills proposed as of June 1994.
SOURCE: Based on survey done by Robert Schwartz and Patricia O'Keefe of McDermott, Will & Emery. Table created by Cynthia A. Beltz and Richard Florida.

100

TABLE A-2
STOCK OF FOREIGN DIRECT INVESTMENT BY COUNTRY AND REGION,
1987–1992
(billions of dollars)

Country or Region	1987	1988	1989	1990	1991	1992[a]
Outward						
France	41	56	75	110	134	151
Germany, F.R.	91	104	122	140	169	186
Japan	78	112	156	204	235	251
United Kingdom	135	172	208	226	244	259
United States	339	353	379	408	438	474
Other	316	372	442	528	579	628
World	1,000	1,169	1,382	1,616	1,799	1,949
Inward						
Developed countries	787	920	1,088	1,260	1,369	
Western Europe	357	419	507	616	702	
North America	342	405	476	528	544	
Other developed	88	96	105	116	123	
Developing countries	212	241	270	300	338	
Africa	22	25	30	32	35	
Latin America and the Caribbean	84	95	104	114	129	
East, South, and Southeast Asia	106	121	136	154	174	
Central and Eastern Europe	0	0	0	0	0	
World	999	1,161	1,357	1,560	1,709	

NOTE: The levels of worldwide inward and outward foreign direct investment stocks should balance; in practice, however, they do not.
a. Estimated.
SOURCE: United Nations, *World Investment Report, 1993: Transnational Corporations and Integrated International Production* (New York: United Nations, 1993), table I.1, p. 14.

TABLE A–3
FOREIGN DIRECT INVESTMENT POSITION, 1980–1990
(billions of dollars)

Industry	1980	1987	1990
Manufacturing			
Industrial inorganic chemicals	6.2	14.6	25.1
Drugs	1.5	5.6	12.4
Computers and office equipment	0.4	1.4	2.7
Audio, video, and communications	1.1	5.2	5.4
Electronic components	1.5	1.3	3.9
Other transportation equipment	0.3	1.2	0.5
Instruments and related products	0.6	4.3	5.7
Services			
Computer and data processing	0.1	0.7	2.3
Engineering and architectural	0.1	3.1	1.2
Total high-tech	11.5	37.5	59.2
All affiliates	83.0	263.4	396.7
High-tech share of total (percent)	14.3	14.9	14.8

SOURCE: U.S. Department of Commerce, "Foreign Direct Investment in the United States: An Update," June 1993.

TABLE A–4
New Work Practices at Japanese Supplier Transplants and U.S. Manufacturing Establishments
(percent)

	Japanese Auto Supplier Transplants	U.S. Establishments			
		Manufacturing plants		All establishments	
		any	less than 50% penetration	any	less than 50% penetration
Teams					
Production	76.7	—	—	—	—
Self-directed	71.2	50.1	32.3	54.5	40.5
Job rotation					
Within teams	82.2	—	—	—	—
Between teams	61.6	55.6	37.4	43.4	26.6
Quality circles					
Current	44.4	45.6	29.7	40.8	27.4
Current or planned	73.6	—	—	—	—
Total quality management	—	44.9	32.1	33.5	24.5
None	12.5	16.0	37.7	21.8	38.6
Teams/rotation/QCs	22.2	N/A	8.4	N/A	7.1

N/A = not available.

NOTE: All figures are expressed as the percent of establishments using the practices indicated.

SOURCES: Richard Florida and Martin Kenney, "Transplanted Organizations: The Transfer of Japanese Industrial Organization to the United States," *American Sociological Review,* vol. 56 (June 1991), pp. 381–98. Paul Osterman, "How Common Is Workplace Transformation and Who Adopts It?" *Industrial and Labor Relations Review,* vol. 47, no. 2 (January 1994).

TABLE A–5
EMPLOYMENT BY U.S. AFFILIATES OF FOREIGN COMPANIES, 1980–1990
(thousands of employees)

Industry	1980	1987	1990
Manufacturing	1,110	1,472	2,097
Mining	61	68	95
Transportation	40	87	223
Wholesale trade	147	282	348
Insurance	61	81	121
Retail trade	372	633	867
Finance, except banking	28	83	64
Real estate	17	31	37
Services	109	329	645
Agriculture	14	18	33
Construction	43	57	70
Communication and public utilities	2	14	27
Other	30	70	79
Total all industries	2,034	3,224	4,705

NOTE: The affiliate data are classified by industry of sales.
SOURCE: U.S. Department of Commerce, Bureau of Economic Analysis, as presented in U.S. Department of Commerce, *Foreign Direct Investment in the United States: An Update* (Washington, D.C.: U.S. Department of Commerce, Economics and Statistics Administration, Office of the Chief Economist, June 1993), table 4A–5, p. 33.

TABLE A–6
JAPANESE EMPLOYMENT AND INVESTMENT IN AUTOMOTIVE-RELATED INDUSTRIES, 1991

Industry	Employment	Investment (millions of dollars)
Automobile assembly	30,080	8,950
Automobile parts	31,860	5,380
Steel	27,418	6,910
Rubber and tires	21,400	5,382
Total	110,758	26,622

SOURCE: Richard Florida.

TABLE A–7
EARNINGS AND WAGES PAID BY JAPANESE TRANSPLANT ASSEMBLERS, 1993

Company	Average Annual Earnings (dollars)	Average Hourly Wages (dollars)	Labor Status
NUMMI	41,545	17.85	Union
Toyota	39,582	16.43	Nonunion
Diamond Star	38,406	17.00	Union
Honda	36,982	16.20	Nonunion
Nissan	36,294	15.62	Nonunion

SOURCE: Richard Florida's compilation from various sources.

TABLE A–8

JAPANESE AUTOMOTIVE R&D AND DESIGN CENTERS IN THE UNITED STATES, 1972–1990

R&D Center	Location	Date Opened	Employment	Major Function
Honda R&D North America, Inc.	Torrance, CA	1975	125	Automotive design
	Marysville, OH	1985	175	Develop prototypes and components; qualify suppliers
Honda Engineering North America	Marysville, OH	1988	180	Design and develop production equipment
Toyota Technical Center USA, Inc.	Gardena, CA	1977	N/A	Vehicle development and testing
	Torrance, CA	1977	82	Prototype testing
	Ann Arbor, MI	1984	48	Evaluate prototype parts; emissions testing
	Southfield, MI	1989	50	Design components and production equipment
	San Francisco, CA	1989	50	Support NUMMI plant
	Lexington, KY	1989	6	Support Georgetown plant
Cally Design Research (Toyota)	Newport Beach, CA	1973	45	Automotive design
Nissan Design International	San Diego, CA	1979	45	Automotive design
Nissan Research & Development	Ann Arbor, MI	1978	N/A	Engine and power train research; emissions testing
	Plymouth, MI	1983	400	Parts engineering for U.S. vehicles
Mazda Research & Development	Irvine, CA	1972	85	Automotive design
	Ann Arbor, MI	1988	20	Engineering research, emissions testing
	Flat Rock, MI	1988	39	Engineering; local parts sourcing
Mitsubishi Design Studio	Cypress, CA	1973	88	Automotive design and engineering
Mitsubishi Motors of America	Southfield, MI	1984	N/A	Joint Chrysler-Mitsubishi development; emissions testing
Isuzu Technical Center	Cerritos, CA	1985	62	Automotive design and testing
	Plymouth, MI	1990	18	Components engineering; emissions testing
Subaru Research and Design	Newport Beach, CA	1986	13	Automotive design
Subaru Technical Center	Garden Grove, CA	1973	65	Develop and test components and vehicles

N/A = not available.

SOURCE: Lindsay Chappel, "The Japanese-American Car," *Automotive News* (November 26, 1990), pp. 42–43.

TABLE A–9
DOMESTIC CONTENT FOR MAJOR JAPANESE VEHICLES PRODUCED IN THE
UNITED STATES, 1991
(percent)

Vehicle	Company	Transplant Facility	Domestic Content
Accord	Honda	Marysville, OH	75.0
Civic	Honda	East Liberty, OH	72.0
Corolla	Toyota	NUMMI, Freemont, CA	75.0
Camry	Toyota	Georgetown, KY	65.0
Sentra	Nissan	Smyrna, TN	74.6
Nissan Pickup	Nissan	Smyrna, TN	57.0
626	Mazda	Flat Rock, MI	65–70
MX-6	Mazda	Flat Rock, MI	65–70
Probe	Mazda (Ford)	Flat Rock, MI	65–70
Eclipse	Mutsubishi	Diamond Star, Normal, IL	60.0
Mirage	Mutsubishi	Diamond Star, Normal, IL	60.0
Rodeo	Isuzu	SIA, Lafayette, IN	73.0
Isuzu Pickup	Isuzu	SIA, Lafayette, IN	65.0
Legacy	Subaru	SIA, Lafayette, IN	53.0

SOURCE: *Automotive News* (March 4, 1991), p. 19.

TABLE A–10
Major Japanese Investments in the U.S. Steel Industry, 1975–1993

Japanese Company	U.S. Partner	Joint Venture Name	Type of Operation	Location	Date	Employment	Investment	Percentage of Japanese Share
Nippon Steel	Inland Steel	I/N Tek	Cold rolling mill	New Carlisle, IN	1990	225	$500 million	40
Nippon Steel	Inland Steel	I/N Kote	Galvanizing line	New Carlisle, IN	1991	100	$600 million	50
Nippon Steel	Inland Steel		Integrated steel mill	Indiana Harbor, IN	1989	11,500	$185 million	14[a]
NKK	National Intergroup	National Steel	Integrated steel mill	Ecorse, MI; Granite, IL; Portage, IN	1984	12,000	$2.2 billion[b]	70
Kawasaki Steel	ARMCO	ARMCO Steel Co., Ltd.	Integrated steel mill	Middletown, OH	1989	9,500	$1.6 billion[c]	45
Kawasaki Steel	ARMCO	ARMCO Steel Co., Ltd.	Galvanizing line	Middletown, OH	1991	100	$150 million	50
Kawasaki Steel	CVRD (Brazil)	California Steel	Rolling mill	Fontana, CA	1984	725	$275 million	50
Kobe Steel	USX Corp.	USS Kobe Steel Co.	Integrated bar and pipe mill	Lorain, OH	1989	3,000	$300 million	50
Kobe Steel	USX Corp.	Protec Coating Co.	Galvanizing line	Leipsic, OH	1992	100	$200 million	50
Sumitomo Metal	LTV Corp.	LSE I	Galvanizing line	Cleveland, OH	1986	83	$100 million	40
Sumitomo Metal	LTV Corp.	LSE II	Galvanizing line	Columbus, OH	1991	100	$180 million	50
Nisshin Steel	Wheeling-Pittsburgh		Integrated steel mill	Steubenville, OH	1988	5,500	$15 million	10[d]
Nisshin Steel	Wheeling-Pittsburgh	Wheeling-Nisshin	Galvanizing and coating line	Follansbee, WV	1988	100	$96 million	67
Nisshin Steel	Wheeling-Pittsburgh	Wheeling-Nisshin	Galvanizing line	Follansbee, WV	1993	100	$120 million	100
Yamato Kogyo	Nucor	Nucor-Yamato	Mini-mill	Blytheville, AR	1988	320	$210 million	50
Kyoei/Sumitomo Corp.		Auburn Steel	Mini-mill	Auburn, NY	1975	315	$300 million	100

NOTE: This table does not include numerous Japanese investments in steel service centers and smaller steel processing facilities.
a. Purchase of 14 percent of Inland Steel stock.
b. $439 million original investment plus $1.8 billion in planned capital improvements.
c. $525 million original investment plus $1.1 billion in planned capital improvements.
d. Purchase of 10 percent Wheeling-Pittsburgh common stock.
SOURCE: Richard Florida.

FIGURE A–1
GLOBAL STOCK OF FOREIGN DIRECT INVESTMENT, BY COUNTRY AND REGION, 1992

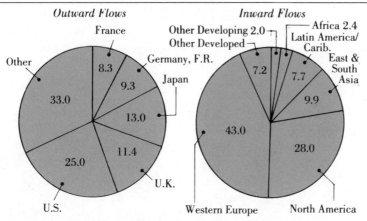

SOURCE: United Nations, *World Investment Report, 1994: Transnational Corporations, Employment, and the Workforce* (New York: United Nations, 1994), table 1.8, p. 19.

FIGURE A–2
INFLOWS OF FOREIGN DIRECT INVESTMENT TO THE UNITED STATES, 1980–1991
(billions of dollars)

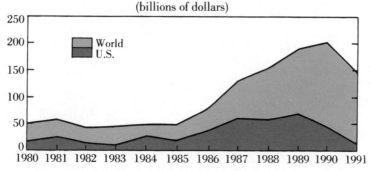

SOURCE: International Monetary Fund, *Balance of Payments Statistics Yearbook*, various issues, as presented in U.S. Department of Commerce, *Foreign Direct Investments in the United States: An Update* (Washington, D.C.: U.S. Department of Commerce, Economics & Statistics Administration, Office of the Chief Economist, June 1993): table 2–1.

FIGURE A–3

INTERNATIONAL INVESTMENT FLOWS FOR THE UNITED STATES, 1988–1993
(billions of dollars)

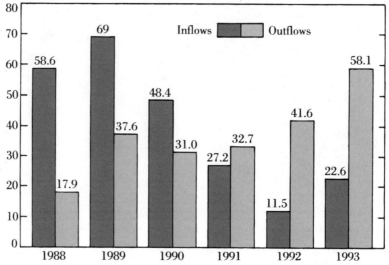

SOURCE: *Survey of Current Business*, August 1992, July 1993, and August 1994.

FIGURE A–4

INTERNATIONAL INVESTMENT AND PRODUCTIVITY

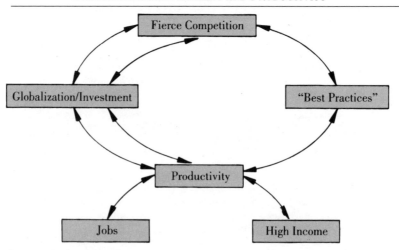

SOURCE: Richard Florida.

FIGURE A–5
AVERAGE VALUE ADDED PER EMPLOYEE, 1980–1991
(thousands of dollars)

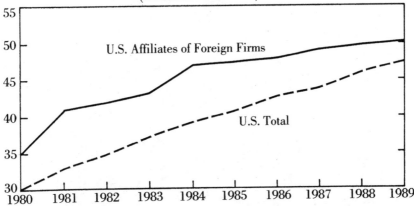

SOURCE: U.S. Department of Commerce, *Foreign Direct Investments in the United States: An Update* (Washington, D.C.: U.S. Department of Commerce, Economics & Statistics Administration, Office of the Chief Economist, June 1993): figure 4A-5, p. 35.

FIGURE A–6
PRODUCTIVITY AND GLOBAL EXPOSURE

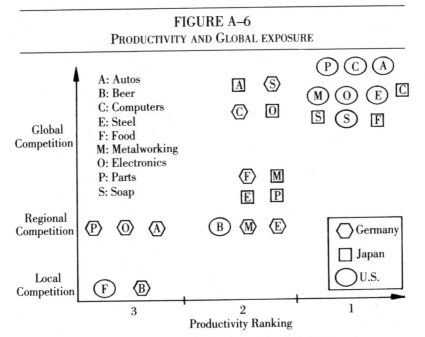

SOURCE: McKinsey Global Institute, Exhibit 3–10, October 1993.

FIGURE A–7

JAPANESE R & D FACILITIES IN THE UNITED STATES

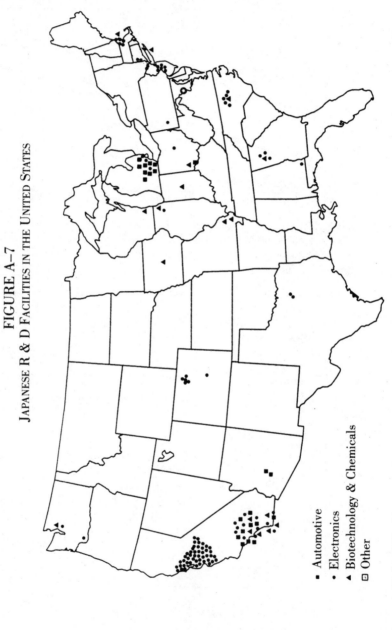

- ■ Automotive
- • Electronics
- ▲ Biotechnology & Chemicals
- ▣ Other

SOURCE: Richard Florida.

FIGURE A–8

FOREIGN R&D EXPENDITURES IN THE UNITED STATES BY COUNTRY,
1980–1990
(billions of dollars)

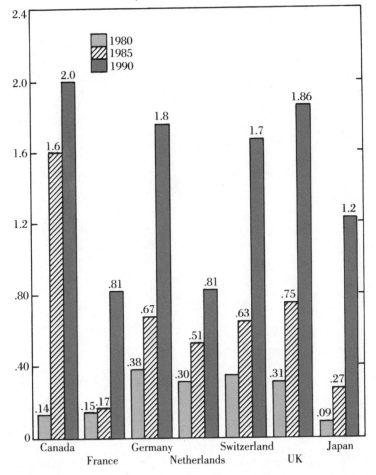

NOTES: Includes foreign direct investment of nonbank U.S. affiliates with 10 percent or more foreign ownership. Excludes expenditures for R&D conducted under a contract. German data are for the former West Germany only.

SOURCE: Bureau of Economic Analysis, "Foreign Direct Investment in the United States," as presented in National Science Foundation, "Science & Engineering Indicators." 1993.

FIGURE A–9
ROYALTY AND LICENSING FEE PAYMENTS AND RECEIPTS BETWEEN U.S.
AFFILIATES AND FOREIGN PARENTS, 1980–1991
(billions of dollars)

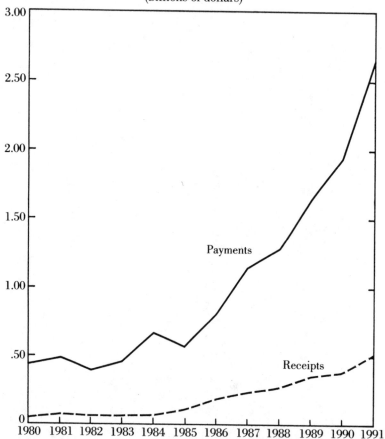

NOTES: Inflows are payments of royalties and license fees by U.S. affiliates to their foreign parents. Outflows are receipts of royalties and license fees by U.S. affiliates from their parent firms. Receipts and payments are before deductions of withholding tax.

SOURCE: Bureau of Economic Analysis, Survey of Current Business, various issues, as presented in U.S. Department of Commerce, *Foreign Direct Investments in the United States: An Update* (Washington, D.C.: U.S. Department of Commerce, Economics & Statistics Administration, Office of the Chief Economist, June 1993): table 6-9, p. 74.

FIGURE A–10

ROYALTY AND LICENSING FEE PAYMENTS AND RECEIPTS, BY SELECTED
COUNTRY OF FOREIGN PARENT, 1991 MANUFACTURING INDUSTRY
(billions of dollars)

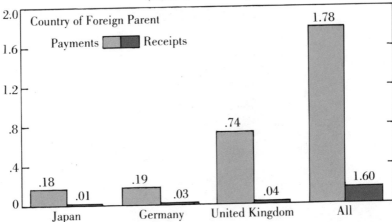

SOURCE: Bureau of Economic Analysis, as presented in U.S. Department of Commerce, *Foreign Direct Investments in the United States: An Update* (Washington, D.C.: U.S. Department of Commerce, Economics & Statistics Administration, Office of the Chief Economist, June 1993), table 6–11.

FIGURE A–11

INTERNATIONAL AFFILIATES' SHARES OF TOTAL U.S. MANUFACTURING
EMPLOYMENT, 1993
(percent)

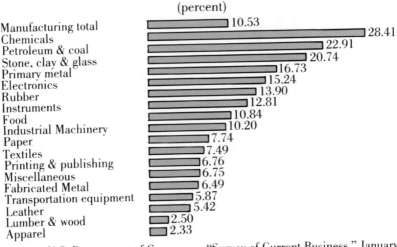

SOURCE: U.S. Department of Commerce, "Survey of Current Business," January 1994, p. 34.

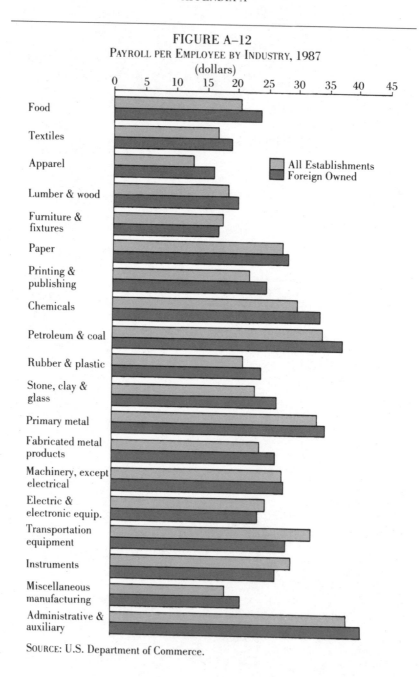

FIGURE A–12
PAYROLL PER EMPLOYEE BY INDUSTRY, 1987
(dollars)

SOURCE: U.S. Department of Commerce.

FIGURE A–13

Japanese Automotive-Related Transplants in the United States

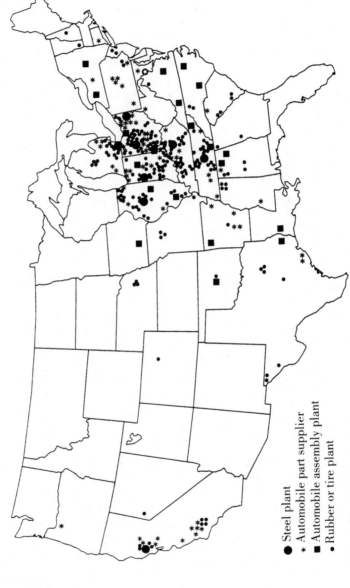

● Steel plant
* Automobile part supplier
■ Automobile assembly plant
• Rubber or tire plant

Source: Richard Florida's database.

117

FIGURE A–14

American, Japanese, and European Television Set and Tube Production in the United States, 1988

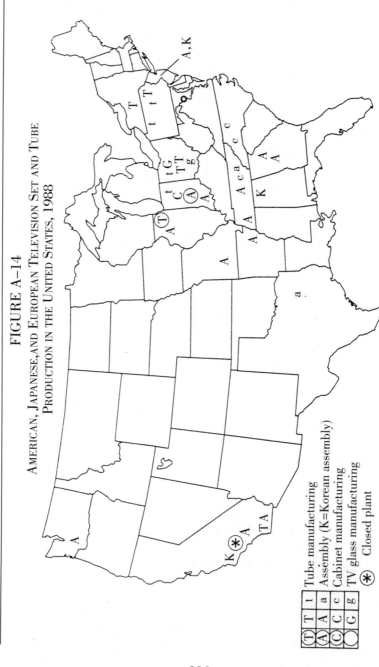

Ⓣ	T	t	Tube manufacturing
Ⓐ	A	a	Assembly (K=Korean assembly)
Ⓒ	C	c	Cabinet manufacturing
Ⓖ	G	g	TV glass manufacturing
⊛	Closed plant		

SOURCE: "Consumer Electronics, HDTV, and the Competitiveness of the U.S. Economy," submitted by EIA's Advanced Television Committee, February 1, 1989.

Provisions in Existing Multilateral Instruments with Significant Impact on FDI

1) World Trade Organization (WTO) Instruments

General Agreement on Trade in Services (GATS). The GATS covers investments in the form of "commercial presence" for the purpose of supplying a service. The benefits of GATS are granted, *inter alia,* to "service suppliers" of another Member. Investment as such is protected to the extent that the service supplier is more than 50 percent owned or controlled by a natural or legal person of another Member. The GATS is the only agreement containing substantial obligations on FDI with potential worldwide coverage (over 100 signatories up to now). It covers all service sectors and its obligations extend to establishment and subsequent operations of the service suppliers of other Members. However, negotiations on important service sectors (financial services, basic telecommunications, maritime transport) are still continuing. Monopolies, government procurement, and subsidies are also covered, but specific disciplines still need to be negotiated.

The central obligations of the GATS are to accord most favored nation treatment for market access (exceptions possible) and national treatment (subject to limitations set out in each Member's schedule of commitments).

The GATS extends obligations to subnational measures, although exceptions regarding state or provincial measures can be inscribed in the schedule. The GATS requires Members to make transparent the measures relating to trade in services. The Agreement provides for compensation in case a liberalization commitment is withdrawn.

One of the most important features of the GATS is the access to the strong state-to-state dispute settlement procedures, including retaliation, agreed upon in the Uruguay Round.

Agreement on Trade-Related Investment Measures (TRIMs). The TRIMs Agreement addresses a number of investment matters from a trade angle, i.e., TRIMS are subject to disciplines because their application distorts trade flows.

The TRIMs Agreement outlaws such TRIMs which are violating Art. III and XI of the General Agreement on Tariffs and Trade 1994. The illustrative list attached to the Agreement includes local content and purchase obligations as well as trade balancing requirements. Such illegal measures can on condition of proper notification be phased out, within two years for developed countries and within up to seven years for least developed countries.

Agreement on Trade-Related Aspects of Intellectual Property Rights (TRIPs). The TRIPs Agreement does not address directly FDI issues, but the improved protection of intellectual property rights brought about by this Agreement will improve the investment climate in the countries concerned.

2) Organization for Economic Cooperation and Development (OECD) Instruments

In 1961, OECD Members have adopted a code of Liberalization of Capital Movements and a Code of Liberalization of Current Invisible Transactions, the so-called Codes of Liberalization, and in 1976 a National Treatment Instrument.

The Codes of Liberalization cover inward direct investment by nonresidents from other Member States, including establishment in services. The National Treatment Instrument comes into play once the foreign direct investment is made and obliges Members, on a non-binding basis, to accord foreign investors and investments national treatment. The OECD members also have adopted non-binding Guidelines for Multinational Enterprises which establish the standards of corporate citizenship for Multinational Enterprises abroad.

The sectoral coverage of the Codes of Liberalization, while comprehensive, is not complete. Countries can maintain individual lists of reservations, be it across the board or in specific sectors. Important issues, such as government procurement, key personnel, subsidies, or monopolies are not covered. To certain commitments a standstill applies and there is a general obligation to reduce restrictions.

The OECD hold regular "country examinations" which amount to a close scrutiny by OECD Committees of the remaining restrictions on FDI maintained by the country concerned. These examinations are to create "peer pressure" aiming at the reduction or withdrawal of restrictions affecting FDI. Besides peer pressure, sanctions for alleged violation of the Codes of Liberalization obligations can only be obtained by referring the issue to the OECD Ministers which could take up the issue in a Council decision in the form of a recommendation. This is no real dispute settlement mechanism, and therefore it is often said that the OECD instruments lack teeth.

3) North American Free Trade Agreement (NAFTA)

The NAFTA contains extensive chapters relating to investment. As a general rule, investors and investments from other Parties are granted the best of most favored nations treatment and national treatment for their establishment and operation. NAFTA Parties are prohibited from applying performance requirements or nationality requirements for key personnel.

It is important to note that these far-reaching basic principles are subject to liberalization commitments and substantial reservations which appear in the Parties' schedules. Each country must also specify non-conforming sub-national measures within a certain time after the entry into force. Government procurement and subsidies are excluded from the general rule; monopolies and state enterprises remain permissible. Financial services are dealt with in a separate chapter. Major exceptions pertain to national security and to Canada's cultural industries.

The NAFTA investment chapter contains a detailed mechanism for the resolution of disputes involving the breach of the NAFTA investment rules by a host country. It provides for investor-to-state dispute settlement.

4) Asia-Pacific Economic Cooperation (APEC)

The APEC annual meeting held in November 1994 agreed on a set of non-binding principles on investment. These "best effort" commitments provide, *inter alia,* for transparency of laws and regulations

121

pertaining to investments; non-discrimination for establishment and operation of investments from any other economy, as well as national treatment, minimization of performance requirements distorting trade and investment; investment protection with regard to expropriation, transfers, and settlement of disputes. An interesting point is that the APEC principles forbid member economics to relax health, safety, and environmental regulations as an incentive to encourage FDI.

The rather general APEC principles are only a first step and work within APEC on more binding investment rules continues.

5) Energy Charter Treaty (ECT)

Signed at Lisbon on December 17, 1994, by almost all European countries, as well as some non-European industrialized countries, this most recent multilateral treaty, covering, *inter alia*, investment, is mainly aimed at Eastern Europe and the CIS. The ECT is a sectoral agreement covering only activities in the energy sector. Its main goal is to facilitate energy related investments in Central and Eastern Europe and to help the restructuring of the sector there. It contains comprehensive rules on investment protection and notably state-of-the-art provisions on trade-related investment measures, key personnel, transfer of funds, sub-national compliance, and an exception clause from the most favored nations obligations for regional integration agreements. It has a refined mechanism for dispute settlement. On pre-investment (market access, right of establishment), only a best-effort commitment for national treatment/most favored national treatment was agreed, but a second phase of negotiations addressing this issue has already started.

6) ACP-EEC Convention of Lomé (Lomé IV)

Lomé IV contains a separate extensive chapter on investments with different sections dealing notably with promotion, protection, financing, capital flows, and payments, as well as establishment. Lomé IV thus notably contains an MFN provision for establishment (unilateral derogations possible) and framework rules for the individual Member States and ACP-countries bilateral investment protection treaties. In addition, the Community in 1992 has elaborated a "Community position on investment protection principles in the ACP states." This detailed document sets out the salient principles which should govern the protection of foreign direct investment in ACP states.

7) United Nations Organization Sponsored Agreements

World Intellectual Property Organization (WIPO). As pointed out above for WTO/TRIPs, the numerous conventions in the area of the protection of intellectual property concluded under the auspices of WIPO do indirectly foster the investment climate in the countries member to these conventions.

International Labor Organization (ILO). The ILO rules on labor standards and labor relations can also be of some importance for international direct investment flows.

Source: Commission of the European Communities, *A Level Playing Field for Direct Investment Worldwide* (Brussels, March 1995).

Notes

CHAPTER 1: INTRODUCTION, *Cynthia A. Beltz*

1. Relative to other countries the United States has few exceptions to this rule. It does restrict foreign investment in areas considered vital for national security, as well as in domestic aviation, banking, and mass communications. Republicans during the 104th session of Congress promised, however, to use their leadership positions to lift some of these restrictions, including the 25 percent ownership restriction under the Federal Communications Act of 1934 on foreign investment in any U.S. communications company. "Pressler Backs Revision of Rules on Ownership of U.S. Telecomm Firms," *International Trade Reporter*, January 4, 1995, p. 11.

2. For liberalization moves among developing countries, see the United Nations, *World Investment Report 1993*, especially pp. 35, 183.

3. Foreign direct investment is the ownership by a foreign person or business of 10 percent or more of the voting securities of an incorporated business enterprise. At the policy level, definitions vary over what investment includes. The United States is pushing in international negotiations for a broad definition that includes not only production but also investments in distribution networks, intellectual property rights, and research activities.

4. United Nations, *World Investment Report 1994: Transnational Corporations, Employment, and the Workplace* (New York: United Nations, 1994), p. 130.

5. Ibid., pp. 130–31.

6. United Nations, *World Investment Report 1993*, p. 126.

7. Robert Lipsey, "Outward Direct Investment and the U.S. Economy," NBER working paper no. 4691, March 1994.

8. For more on the theory of foreign-market penetration through FDI and the problem of structural impediments, see papers from "Foreign Direct Investment into Japan: Why So Small and How To Encourage?" U.S.-Japan Management Studies Center, the Wharton School of the University of Pennsylvania, October 6–7, 1994.

9. United Nations, *World Investment Report 1994*.

10. Under the Trade Related Investment Measures (TRIMs) in the Uruguay Round Agreement, local content restrictions are prohibited for the first time at a multilateral level. But a comprehensive code that includes a broad national treatment commitment and protection of investment is still being developed through forums such as the Organization for Economic Cooperation and Development and the forum on Asia Pacific Economic Cooperation.

11. Stephen Canner, U.S. Department of Treasury office director for international investment, testimony before the Defense Policy Panel and Investigations Subcommittee of the Armed Services Committee, U.S. House of Representatives, May 14, 1992.

12. See U.S. Congress Office of Technology Assessment, *Multinationals and the National Interest: Playing by Different Rules* (Washington, D.C.: U.S. Government Printing Office, September 1993), as well as *Multinationals and the U.S. Technolo-*

125

gy Base (Washington, D.C.: U.S. Government Printing Office, October 1994), especially pp. 4, 25–27, 33.

13. Robert Schwartz and Bennett Caplan, "Conditioning the Unconditional," *New York Law Journal*, August 19, 1994.

14. Diffuse reciprocity, in contrast to specific reciprocity, is consistent with the principle of nondiscrimination. See Robert Keohane, "Reciprocity in International Relations," *International Organization*, vol. 40, Winter 1986.

15. Office of Technology Assessment, *Multinationals and the U.S. Technology Base*, 1994, p. 28.

16. Robin Gaster and Clyde V. Prestowitz, *Shrinking the Atlantic: Europe and the American Economy* (Washington, D.C.: The Economic Strategy Institute, June 1994) recommends that European investment in the United States be given priority because of the "shared" views between the United States and the European Union as opposed to the economic views of countries in the Pacific Rim.

17. Office of Technology Assessment, *Multinationals and the National Interest*, 1993, p. 43.

18. See, for example, the Chamber of Commerce letter to the Secretary of Commerce dated October 8, 1993.

19. See Secretary Ronald H. Brown letter to Sen. John D. Dingell, answer to question eight, June 15, 1994.

20. Instead Clinton has said that although the United States will welcome foreign investment in our businesses, "we insist that our investors should be *equally* welcome in other countries." Speech given at American University, February 26, 1993.

CHAPTER 2: FOREIGN INVESTORS MAKE LOUSY CROWBARS, *Cynthia A. Beltz*

1. This chapter is in part based on two *Upside* articles, "Don't Stifle Foreign Investment," July 1994, and " 'Buy U.S.' Rules Can Backfire," September 1994.

2. Alexander Kenneth Hamilton, Report to Congress on Manufacturers (1791), cited in K. Crowe, *America for Sale* (Garden City, N.Y.: Doubleday, 1978), p. 249.

3. U.S. Trade Representative, *Annual Report of the President of the United States on the Trade Agreements: 1983* (Washington, D.C.: U.S. Government Printing Office, 1982), p. 174.

4. *Economic Report of the President,* February 1991 (Washington, D.C.: U.S. Government Printing Office, 1991), p. 262.

5. U.S. investment obligations are also contained in the OECD Code of Liberalization and Capital Movements, the Uruguay Round Agreement on Trade Related Investment Measures, and the General Agreement on Trade in Services. See Kenneth J. Vandevelde, "The Bilateral Investment Treaty Program of the United States," *Cornell International Law Journal*, vol. 21, 1988, pp. 202–276. José Alvarez, "Political Protectionism and U.S. Investment Obligations in Conflict: The Hazards of Exon-Florio," *Virginia Journal of International Law*, vol. 30, Fall 1989; Harvey E. Bale, "The U.S. Policy Toward Inward Foreign Direct Investment," *Vanderbilt Journal of Transnational Law*, vol. 18, Spring 1985, pp. 199–222.

6. Office of Technology Assessment, *Multinationals and the National Interest: Playing by Different Rules*, OTA-ITE-569 (Washington, D.C.: U.S. Government Printing Office, September 1993), pp. 17–18.

7. Stephen Krasner, "Trade Conflicts and the Common Defense: The United States and Japan," *Political Science Quarterly*, vol. 101, 1986, p. 789. See also the National Academy of Engineering, *Foreign Participation in U.S. Research and Development: Asset or Liability?* (forthcoming, 1995).

8. Linda Spencer, *Foreign Investment in the United States: Unencumbered Access* (The Economic Strategy Institute, May 1991).

9. Clyde V. Prestowitz, Jr., et al., *The Future of the Airline Industry* (Economic Strategy Institute, July 1993).

10. Robert Reich, "Who Is Us?" *Harvard Business Review*, January 1990, pp. 53–64; Laura D'Andrea Tyson, "They Are Not Us: Why American Ownership Still Matters," *The American Prospect*, vol. 4, Winter 1990, pp. 37–48; Stephen Thomsen, "We Are Us," *The Columbia Journal of World Business*, Winter 1992, pp. 6–14.

11. Laura D'Andrea Tyson, testimony to the U.S. Senate Subcommittee on International Finance and Monetary Policy of the Committee on Banking, Foreign Acquisition of U.S.-Owned Companies (Washington, D.C.: U.S. Government Printing Office, 1992), 102nd Congress, second session, pp. 75–76.

12. For more detail on Exon-Florio as an investment barrier, see Alvarez, "Political Protectionism," p. 89.

13. On Commerce Secretary Baldridge's opposition to the Fairchild sale because of the problem of market access in Japan, see Donna K. H. Walters and Williams C. Rempel, "Trade War Victim," *Los Angeles Times*, December 1, 1987; David E. Sanger, "Japanese Purchase of Chip Maker Canceled after Objections in United States," *New York Times*, March 17, 1987; also, Norman Glickman and Douglas P. Woodward, *The New Competitors: How Foreign Investors Are Changing the U.S. Economy* (New York: Basic Books, 1989), pp. 267–69.

14. Alvarez, "Political Protectionism," pp. 8–12. Bills included S.2028, introduced by Senator Riegle, 101st Congress, second session (1990) on financial services; H.R.3699, introduced by Rep. Campbell, 101st Congress, first session (1989) on amending 1974 Trade Act; and H.R.2643, introduced by Rep. Markey, 101st Congress, first session (1989) on foreign ownership of cable television systems.

15. Michael Borrus, "Who Is Us? Foreign Participation in U.S.-Funded R&D," a Berkeley Roundtable on International Economics Research Note, July 9, 1994. Office of Technology Assessment, *Multinationals and the National Interest*, 1993.

16. Irwin Stelzer, "New Protectionism," *National Review*, March 16, 1992, pp. 30–34.

17. R. Michael Gadbaw, "Reciprocity and Its Implications for U.S. Trade Policy, *Law and Policy in International Business*, vol. 14, 1982, especially pp. 701–14.

18. William Diebold, Jr., *Bilateralism, Multilateralism, and Canada in U.S. Trade Policy* (Cambridge: Ballinger Publishing Company, 1988), p. 11.

19. Under section 301 of the 1974 Trade Act, the U.S. Trade Representative is authorized to take appropriate action against "unreasonable" or "discriminatory" practices of a foreign country that restricts U.S. commerce, which is explicitly defined to include foreign direct investment by U.S. persons. Trade Act of 1974, 19 U.S.C. 2411; Pub. L. No. 93-618 (codified as amended by P.L. 96-39, P.L. 98-573, and P.L. 100-418), Title III, Chap. 1, Sec. 301 (b) (1) and (d) (1).

20. The United States did cite India, for example, under section 301 for its 40 percent limitation on foreign equity ownership and its performance requirements,

but it then chose not to retaliate under the law. "U.S. Will Not Retaliate Against India under Super 301," *International Trade Reporter*, 1990, p. 893.

21. On managed trade tactics, see Jagdish Bhagwati, ed., *Aggressive Unilateralism;* Robert Keohane, "Reciprocity in International Relations"; Yarbrough and Yarbrough, "Reciprocity, Bilateralism, and Economic Hostages: Self-enforcing Agreements in International Trade," in *International Studies Quarterly*, 1986, v. 30, pp. 7–21; and Jagdish Bhagwati and Douglas A. Irwin, "The Return of the Reciprocitarians—U.S. Trade Policy Today," *The World Economy*, June 1987.

22. Robert S. Schwartz and Bennett A. Caplan, "Conditioning the Unconditional," *New York Law Journal*, August 19, 1993.

23. Bhagwati, *Aggressive Unilateralism*, pp. 3, 206.

24. Diebold, *Bilateralism, Multilateralism, and Canada*, p. 15.

25. Sir James Graham, in 1849, as cited by Keohane, "Reciprocity in International Relations," p. 15.

26. Alvarez, "Political Protectionism," p. 12.

27. Cynthia Beltz, "Lessons from the Cutting Edge and HDTV," *Regulation*, February 1994; and *High-Tech Maneuvers: The Industrial Policy Lessons of HDTV* (Washington, D.C.: AEI Press, 1992).

28. Rachel McCulloch, "Foreign Investment in the U.S.: Source of Strength or Sign of Weakness?" *Economic Directives*, vol. 3, June 1993, p. 6.

29. McKinsey Global Institute, *Manufacturing Productivity* (Washington, D.C., October 1993), pp. 4–5 and Exhibit 3–10.

30. Department of Commerce 1993, pp. 62, 70.

31. Cletus C. Coughlin, "Foreign-owned Companies in the United States: Malign or Benign?" *Federal Reserve Bank of St. Louis Review*, May/June 1992, pp. 17–31. U.S. Department of Commerce, 1993.

32. Douglas C. Worth, remarks of the chairman of the Trade Committee, Business and Industry Advisory Committee to the OECD Roundtable, on the New Dimensions of Market Access in a Globalized World Economy, June 30–July 1, 1994.

33. Schwartz and Caplan, "Conditioning the Unconditional"; Agnes P. Dover, deputy general counsel, U.S. Department of Energy at the National Research Council, "International Access to National Technology Promotion Programs," January 19, 1995.

34. Office of Technology Assessment, 1993, p. 19.

35. Susan W. Liebeler and William H. Lash III, "Exon-Florio: Harbinger of Economic Nationalism?" *Regulation*, Winter 1993, pp. 44–51. Alvarez, "Political Protectionism," p. 89.

36. On determinants of relative bargaining power under a tit-for-tat strategy, see John McMillan, "Strategic Bargaining and Section 301," in Bhagwati, *Aggressive Unilateralism*, pp. 207–09.

37. United Nations, *World Investment Report 1994*, pp. 4, 17.

38. AT&T comments cited in July 22, 1994, letter, p. 7 from fourteen major industry associations that opposed the Manton amendment, including the National Association of Manufacturers and the American Electronics Association.

39. For example, much of Japanese R&D is not funded through the government. On the other problems associated with quick government remedies to increase FDI (business structures, factor costs, cultural differences), see papers sponsored by The U.S.-Japan Management Studies Center for the conference "Foreign Direct

Investment into Japan: Why So Small and How to Encourage?" October 7, 1994, the Wharton School of the University of Pennsylvania.

40. See the letter from Secretary Ronald Brown to the House Committee on Energy and Commerce and Chairman John D. Dingell, dated June 15, 1994, answer to question six.

41. Keohane, "Reciprocity in International Relations," p. 13.

42. Francis Bowes Sayre, *The Way Forward: The American Trade Agreements Program* (New York: MacMillan Company, 1939), p. 109.

43. Letter to Secretary of State Hughes, December 14, 1922, reprinted in William S. Culbertson, *Reciprocity: A National Policy for Foreign Trade* (New York: McGraw-Hill Book Company, 1937), p. 246.

44. Letter from Charles Evans Hughes to Senator Henry Cabot Lodge, March 13, 1924, reprinted in John T. Bill Co. v. United States, 104 F.2d 67, 72 (C.C.P.A. 1939).

45. Jacob Viner, "The Most Favored Nation Clause in American Commercial Treaties," originally published in *The Journal of Political Economy*, vol. 32, February 1924; reprinted in *International Economics* (Glencoe, Illinois: Free Press, 1954), p. 25.

46. Keohane, "Reciprocity in International Relations," p. 19.

47. Paul Bryan Christy III, "Negotiating Investment in the GATT: A Call for Functionalism," *Michigan Journal of International Law*, Summer 1991. A. Fatourous, ed., *Transnational Corporations: The International Legal Framework*, the United Nations Library on Transnational Corporations (London: Routledge), 1994.

48. Guy de Jonquieres, "Britain Wants WTO Rules for Investment," *Financial Times*, January 19, 1995.

49. United Nations, *World Investment Report 1994*, pp. 124, 284.

50. There are forty-three signatories to the former Standard Code, but under the World Trade Organization, adherence to the code will be mandatory for all members. The Uruguay Round Agreement expands the openness and transparency requirements of the existing code (the 1980 Agreement on Technical Barriers to Trade) to include all conformity procedures used to determine if a product complies with a technical regulation. The agreement also extends some of the Standard Code's transparency requirements beyond the national government to the state level. See Brown letter to Dingell, answers to questions six and seven.

51. United Nations, *World Investment Report 1994*, p. 124, and the *World Investment Report 1992*, p. 336.

52. United Nations, *World Investment Report 1994*, p. 51.

53. A weak, tentative step was taken toward multilateral rules in the November 1994 annual meeting. For a critical assessment of APEC investment principles that were included in the November agreement, see the letter from the U.S. Council for International Business to the U.S. Trade Representative's office, June 28, 1994.

54. See Brown letter to Dingell, answer to question seven.

55. United Nations, *World Investment Report 1994*, p. 59. See also, United Nations, *World Investment Report 1993*, p. 107–08.

56. Harris Research, *The European Business Monitor*, phase 4, conducted September 5 through October 17, 1994, as cited by David Marsh, "European Business Leaders Apprehensive of Growing Economic Power of Asian Nations," *Financial Times*, November 17, 1994.

57. See remarks of Douglas C. Worth, June 30–July 1, 1994, p. 4.

58. Schwartz and Caplan, "Conditioning the Unconditional."

59. Alvarez, "Political Protectionism."

CHAPTER 3: CONDITIONING INVESTMENT IS A LOSING STRATEGY, *Richard Florida*

1. McKinsey Global Institute, *Manufacturing Productivity* (Washington, D.C., October 1993).

2. Organization for Economic Cooperation and Development (OECD), *Performance of Foreign Affiliates in OECD Countries* (Paris: OECD, September 1994).

3. Richard Florida and Martin Kenney, "The Globalization of Japanese R&D," *Economic Geography* (1994).

4. Martin Kenney and Richard Florida, *Beyond Mass Production: The Japanese System and Its Transfer* (Oxford: Oxford University Press, 1993).

5. Richard Florida and Martin Kenney, "Restructuring in Place: Japanese Investment, Production, Organization, and the Geography of Steel," *Economic Geography*, vol. 68, no. 2 (April 1992), pp. 146–73.

6. Richard Florida, "The Economic Transformation of the Industrial Midwest" (Center for Economic Development, Carnegie Mellon University, August 1994).

CHAPTER 4: NOT ALL INVESTMENT IS THE SAME, *Clyde V. Prestowitz, Jr.*

1. Clyde V. Prestowitz, Jr., et al., *The Future of the Airline Industry* (Washington, D.C.: Economic Strategy Institute, July 1993), table 7.1, p. 28.

2. Ibid., p. 35.

CHAPTER 5: NEGOTIATE, DON'T LEGISLATE RECIPROCITY, *Daniel M. Price*

1. The Manton amendment, attached to the House version of the National Competitiveness Act, passed the House in May 1993. The Senate opposed the Manton amendment, approving an alternative clause that required "that the principal economic benefits accrue to the domestic economy of the United States." This compromise did not prevail in the conference committee, and in the end, the whole bill had to be withdrawn.

CHAPTER 6: USE A DIFFERENT LEVER, *Ellen L. Frost*

1. Letter from Secretary of Commerce Ronald H. Brown to Senator John D. Dingell, June 15, 1994.

2. TRIMs are typically associated with two objectives: first, to influence location and pattern of economic activity; and second, to capture a greater share of benefits from a multinational firm's activities for the domestic economy, including trade balancing requirements.

3. APEC is a forum established in 1989 that includes seventeen Asia-Pacific economies, with a small secretariat in Singapore.

4. Under a Presidential Executive Order of March 3, 1994, the U.S. Trade Representative must identify, in 1994 and 1995, those "priority foreign country practices," the elimination of which will have the greatest potential for the expansion of U.S. exports.

CHAPTER 7: HOW DO WE MOVE FORWARD?

1. The United States can also influence China by conditioning support for its application to international economic organizations for membership. Mickey Kantor has said, for example, that the United States supports China's bid to join the GATT and the World Trade Organization but not until China meets world standards for enforcement of intellectual property. For more details, see "China Cited under Special 301 Law," *International Trade Reporter*, July 6, 1994, p. 1066.

CHAPTER 8: FOREIGN DIRECT INVESTMENT AND THE ECONOMY, *Richard Florida*

This chapter was prepared for the American Enterprise Institute, the Program for Trade and Technology, where Cynthia Beltz and Claude Barfield provided support and helpful comments. Comments were also provided by Douglas Irwin, Bennett Caplan, Todd Malan, Donald Smith, and David Jenkins. J. David Lasher, Demetrius Kydoniefs, Rafael Vesga, Christopher Berdnik, and Eaen McCarthy provided research assistance, and Sandra Salmonsen provided technical support.

1. See United Nations, *World Investment Report: Transnational Corporations and Integrated International Production* (New York: United Nations, 1993).

2. For a more thorough discussion of U.S. policy toward international investment, see David Bailey, George Harte, and Roger Sugden, "U.S. Policy Debate toward Inward Investment," *Journal of World Trade*, vol. 26 (August 1992), pp. 65–93.

3. See Theodore Moran, "The Impact of TRIMs on Trade and Development," *Transnational Corporations*, vol. 1, no. 1 (February 1992), pp. 55–66.

4. See Edward Graham and Paul Krugman, *Foreign Direct Investment in the United States* (Washington, D.C.: Institute for International Economics, 1991).

5. James K. Jackson, "Foreign Direct Investment in the United States" (Washington, D.C.: U.S. Library of Congress, Congressional Research Service, CRS Report IB93011, 1993), p. 4.

6. Ibid., p. 6.

7. For a more thorough discussion of Exon-Florio, see Ellison F. McCoy, "The Reauthorization of Exon-Florio: A Battle between Spurring the U.S. Economy and Protecting National Security," *Georgia Journal of International and Comparative Law*, vol. 22 (Fall 1992), pp. 685–700.

8. Jackson, "Foreign Direct Investment," p. 7.

9. For a more thorough discussion of conditional national treatment, see Bennett A. Caplan and Robert S. Schwartz, "Conditioning the Unconditional," *New York Law Journal* (August 19, 1993).

10. U.S. Congress, Office of Technology Assessment, *Multinationals and the National Interest: Playing by Different Rules* (Washington, D.C.: U.S. Government Printing Office, September 1993).

11. See European Parliament, Committee on Economic and Monetary Affairs, *Draft Report on the State of the European Electronics Industry* (November 12, 1993).

12. Robert Reich, "Who Is Us?" *Harvard Business Review* (January–February 1990). Reich, *The Work of Nations* (New York: Knopf, 1991).

13. Laura Tyson, *Who's Bashing Whom? Trade Conflicts in High-Technology Industries* (Washington, D.C.: Institute for International Economics, November 1992).

14. Keith Bradsher, "In Shift, White House Will Stress Aiding Foreign Concerns in U.S.," *New York Times* (June 2, 1993).

15. Economic Strategy Institute, *Foreign Investment in the United States: Unencumbered Access* (Washington, D.C.: Economic Strategy Institute, 1991); Economic Strategy Institute, *The Future of the Airline Industry* (Washington, D.C.: Economic Strategy Institute, 1993); Economic Strategy Institute, *Shrinking the Atlantic: Europe and the American Economy* (Washington, D.C.: Economic Strategy Institute, 1994).

16. United Nations, *World Investment Report 1993: Transnational Corporations and Integrated International Production* (New York: United Nations, 1993).

17. The largest component of the growth in U.S. international investment came not surprisingly from Japan. Japanese international investment in the United States more than doubled between 1985 and 1991, and it accounted for nearly one-third (30 percent) of the total increase over this period. The largest international investor in the United States, however, remains the United Kingdom, with 26 percent of the total. Taken together, the major European countries account for more than 50 percent. U.S. Department of Commerce, *Foreign Direct Investment in the United States* (June 1993), p. 19.

18. Ibid.

19. See Ned Howenstine and William Zeile, "Characteristics of Foreign-Owned U.S. Manufacturing Establishments," *Survey of Current Business* (January 1994), pp. 36–38.

20. Sylvia E. Bargas and Jeffrey Lowe, "Direct Investment Positions on a Historical-Cost Basis, 1993," *Survey of Current Business*, June 1994, p. 73.

21. U.S. Department of Commerce, *Survey of Current Business* (various issues and unpublished data).

22. There are three components of international investment: amount of equity inflows, changes in intercompany debt, and reinvested earnings. According to Department of Commerce data, all three fell sharply in the early 1990s. Net equity investments fell by $35 billion between 1989 and 1992, reinvested earnings declined to $6 billion, and intercompany debt flows dropped by $31 billion. See U.S. Department of Commerce, *Foreign Direct Investment in the United States* (June 1993) and *Survey of Current Business* (August 1994).

23. U.S. Department of Commerce, *Foreign Direct Investment in the United States* (June 1993), p. 25.

24. In contrast to the rapid growth of the late 1980s, world international investment outflows fell sharply in 1991. World international investment outflows peaked at $235 billion and declined to $183 billion in 1991. Japanese outward international investment declined from $48 billion in 1990 to $30.7 billion in 1991, a drop of 36 percent. For the Japanese, this was a result of recession. See JETRO, *JETRO White Paper on Foreign Direct Investment: The Slowdown in Direct Investment and How Companies Are Dealing with It* (Tokyo: JETRO, March 1993).

25. See World Bank, *The East Asian Miracle: Economic Growth and Public Policy* (New York: University Press, 1993). Also see, Robert Wade, *Governing the Mar-*

ket: Economic Theory and the Role of Government in the East Asian Industrialization (Princeton: Princeton University Press, 1990).

26. Concise and readable synopses of the literature on international investment can be found in Robert Gilpin, *The Political Economy of International Relations* (Princeton: Princeton University Press, 1987), especially chapter 6; and Edward Graham and Paul Krugman, *Foreign Direct Investment in the United States* (Washington, D.C.: Institute for International Economics, 1991). DeAnne Julius, "Foreign Direct Investment: The Neglected Twin of Trade" (Washington, D.C.: Group of Thirty, Occasional Papers, no. 33, 1991), does a good job of situating the theory of international investment with relation to trade theory. See Richard Caves, *Multinational Enterprise and Economic Analysis* (Cambridge: Cambridge University Press, 1982) for a more complete review of work in this field.

27. See Raymond Vernon, "International Investment and International Trade in the Product Cycle," *Quarterly Journal of Economics*, vol. 83, no. 1, pp. 190–207; and Vernon, *Sovereignty at Bay* (New York: Basic Books, 1971).

28. See Stephen Hymer, *The International Operations of National Firms* (Cambridge, Mass.: MIT Press, 1976). Also see Folker Froebel, Jurgen Heinrichs, and Otto Kreye, *The New International Division of Labor* (Cambridge: Cambridge University Press, 1980).

29. See, for example, Peter Buckley and Mark Casson, *The Future of Multinational Enterprise* (London: MacMillan, 1976).

30. See Oliver Williamson, *Markets and Hierarchies* (New York: Free Press, 1975); David Teece, *The Multinational Corporation and the Resource Cost of International Technology Transfer* (Cambridge, Mass.: Ballinger, 1976); Teece, "Transactions Cost Economics and the Multinational Enterprise: An Assessment," *Journal of Economic Behavior and Organization*, vol. 7 (1986); Mark Casson, "Transactions Costs and the Theory of the Multinational Enterprise," in Alan Rugman, ed., *Theories of MNEs* (London: Croom Helm, 1982), pp. 24–43.

31. See John Dunning, *International Production and the Multinational Enterprise* (London: Allen and Unwin, 1981); and Dunning, *Multinationals, Technology, and Competitiveness* (London: Unwin Hyman, 1988).

32. Michael Porter, *The Competitive Advantage of Nations* (New York: Free Press, 1990); and Michael Porter, ed., *Competition in Global Industries* (Boston: Harvard Business School Press, 1986). Also see Christopher Bartlett and Sumantra Ghoshal, *Managing Across Borders: The Transnational Solution* (Boston: Harvard Business School Press, 1989). An interesting review of Porter's framework for international investment and the theory of the multinational firm is provided in John Dunning, "The Competitive Advantage of Countries and the Activities of Transnational Corporations," *Transnational Corporations*, vol. 1, no. 1 (February 1992), pp. 135–68.

33. See, for example, Stephen Hymer, "The Multinational Corporation and the Law of Uneven Development," in Jagdish Bhagwati, ed., *Economics and World Order* (New York: Free Press, 1972); and Raymond Vernon, *Sovereignty at Bay* (New York: Basic Books, 1971).

34. For a series of recent articles and a recently published book on this issue, see Paul Krugman, "Competitiveness: A Dangerous Obsession," *Foreign Affairs* (March/April 1994), pp. 28–44; Paul Krugman, *Peddling Prosperity* (New York:

W.W. Norton, 1994); and Paul Krugman and Robert Lawrence, "Trade, Jobs, and Wages," *Scientific American* (April 1994) pp. 44–49.

35. McKinsey Global Institute, *Manufacturing Productivity* (Washington, D.C., October 1993).

36. From McKinsey Global Institute, *Manufacturing Productivity* (1993), as quoted in the *Wall Street Journal* (October 27, 1993).

37. Organization for Economic Cooperation and Development, *Performance of Foreign Affiliates in the OECD Countries* (Paris: OECD, September 1994); also see Robert Keatley, "OECD Says Foreign Investment Is Good for You," *Dow Jones/Wall Street Journal Electronic News Service* (April 8, 1994).

38. See Howenstine and Zeile, "Characteristics of Foreign-Owned U.S. Manufacturing Establishments," p. 48.

39. U.S. Department of Commerce, *Foreign Direct Investment in the United States* (June 1993), p. 32.

40. See U.S. Department of Commerce, *FDI in the U.S.: Review and Analysis of Current Developments* (August 1991), p. 35. Also see European-American Chamber of Commerce, *Jobs and Investments of European Firms Operating in the United States* (Washington, D.C., March 1993).

41. Richard Florida and Martin Kenney, "Transplanted Organizations: The Transfer of Japanese Industrial Organization to the United States," *American Sociological Review*, vol. 56 (June 1991), pp. 381–90.

42. See Paul Osterman, "How Common Is Workplace Transformation and Who Adopts It?" *Industrial and Labor Relations Review*, vol. 47, no. 2 (January 1994).

43. See Richard Florida and Martin Kenney, "Restructuring in Place: Japanese Investment, Production Organization, and the Geography of Steel," *Economic Geography*, vol. 68, no. 2 (April 1992), pp. 146–73.

44. See Richard Florida and Martin Kenney, "The Globalization of Japanese R&D," *Economic Geography* (1994, forthcoming); Donald Dalton and Manuel Serapio, *U.S. Research Facilities of Foreign Companies* (Washington, D.C.: U.S. Department of Commerce, Technology Administration, Japan Technology Program, January 1993).

45. See U.S. Department of Commerce, *Foreign Direct Investment in the United States* (June 1993), p. 70.

46. A recent report by the European-American Chamber of Commerce notes that the European affiliated research, development, and design centers "spend significantly higher amounts of U.S. R&D than U.S. manufacturing firms as a whole . . . and have an excellent track record for R&D achievements," highlighting U.S. research by SmithKline and Hoechst Celanese that has led to the development of new drugs; BP America's efforts in "green R&D"; ICI America's work on herbicide-tolerant crops; Thomson's extensive U.S. research in consumer electronics; BASF's state-of-the-art automotive coatings lab in North Carolina; Philips's world-class lighting research center in New Jersey; and Siemens's extensive U.S. efforts as being particularly notable. See European-American Chamber of Commerce, *Jobs and Investments of European Firms Operating in the United States* (Washington, D.C., March 1993).

47. U.S. Department of Commerce, *Foreign Direct Investment in the United States* (June 1993), p. 73.

48. Norman Glickman and Douglas Woodward, *The New Competitors: How Foreign Investors Are Changing the U.S. Economy* (New York: Basic Books, 1989).

49. U.S. General Accounting Office, *Foreign Investment: Growing Japanese Presence in the U.S. Auto Industry* (Washington, D.C., March 1988).

50. U.S. General Accounting Office, *Foreign Investment: Japanese-Affiliated Automakers' 1989 U.S. Production's Impact on Jobs* (Washington, D.C., October 1990).

51. UAW, "Transplants and Job Loss: The UAW Response to the General Accounting Office," *UAW Research Bulletin* (May 1988).

52. See Candace Howes, *Japanese Auto Transplants and the U.S. Automobile Industry* (Washington, D.C.: Economic Policy Institute, 1993).

53. "Japanese Carmakers Are Coddling Their U.S. Kids," *Business Week* (March 4, 1991), p. 21.

54. *Business Week* (May 30, 1994).

55. Graham and Krugman, *Foreign Direct Investment in the United States*, p. 61.

56. See Howenstine and Zeile, "Characteristics of Foreign-Owned U.S. Manufacturing Establishments," p. 45.

57. See Donald F. Smith, Jr., and Richard Florida, "Agglomeration and Industrial Location: An Econometric Analysis of Japanese-Affiliated Manufacturers in Automotive-related Industries," *Journal of Urban Economics* (1994).

58. See Kenney and Florida, *Beyond Mass Production*.

59. Graham and Krugman, *Foreign Direct Investment in the United States*, p. 70.

60. See Lindsay Chappell, "Fuji Considering Plan for U.S. Engine Plant," *Automotive News* (November 13, 1989), p. 2; and Louise Kertesz, "Diamond Star Execs Consider Engine Plant for 1992–1994," *Automotive News* (July 31, 1989), p. 10.

61. See *UAW Research Bulletin* (November 1989).

62. See Kenney and Florida, *Beyond Mass Production*.

63. See Richard Florida and Martin Kenney, "The Japanese Transplants: Production Organization and Regional Development," *Journal of the American Planning Association* (Winter 1992), pp. 21–38.

64. Richard Florida and Martin Kenney, "Restructuring in Place: Japanese Investment, Production Organization, and the Geography of Steel," *Economic Geography*, vol. 68, no. 2 (April 1992), pp. 146–73.

65. On the economic transformation of the Industrial Midwest, see Richard Florida, "The Economic Transformation of the Industrial Midwest" (Pittsburgh, Penn.: Center for Economic Development, Carnegie Mellon University, August 1994). Also see Council of Great Lakes Governors, *North America's High-Performance Heartland* (Chicago, Ill.: Council of Great Lakes Governors, May 1994); Richard Florida et al., *Reinventing the Heartland: A High-Performance Strategy for the Great Lakes Region* (Report to the Council of Great Lakes Governors, June 1993); Richard Florida et al., *Rebuilding America: Lessons from the Industrial Heartland* (Report to the Council of Great Lakes Governors, December 1992).

66. See Federal Reserve Bank of Chicago, *Annual Report, 1994* (Chicago, 1994).

67. This section is drawn from a site visit to Battle Creek and personal interviews with James F. Hettinger, president and CEO, Battle Creek Unlimited, Battle Creek, Michigan; and corporate officials from Nippondenso, Koyo Metals, Technical Auto Parts, October 1990. Also see a case study of Battle Creek Unlimited, Lyke Thomson, "The Politics of Economic Development: A Qualitative Case Study," *Economic Development Review* (Summer 1984), pp. 62–68.

68. See Organization for Economic Cooperation and Development, Directorate for Financial, Fiscal, and Enterprise Affairs, Committee on International Investment and Multinational Enterprises, Working Group on Investment Policies and the Guidelines, *Feasibility Study of a Wider Investment Instrument* (Paris: OECD, August 1993).

A NOTE ON THE BOOK

This book was edited by Cheryl Weissman
of the AEI Press.
The text was set in Bodoni by
Publication Technology Corporation,
of Fairfax, Virginia.
Data Reproducers Corporation,
of Rochester Hills, Michigan,
printed and bound the book,
using permanent acid-free paper.

The AEI Press is the publisher for the American Enterprise Institute for Public Policy Research, 1150 17th Street, N.W., Washington, D.C. 20036: *Christopher C. DeMuth,* publisher; *Dana Lane,* director; *Ann Petty,* editor; *Leigh Tripoli,* editor; *Cheryl Weissman,* editor; *Lisa Roman,* editorial assistant (rights and permissions).